# The Cowbell Principle

## Career Advice On How To Get Your Dream Job And Make More Money

BRIAN CARTER
GARRISON WYNN

# DEDICATION

Garrison dedicates this book to all the people who feel they have success trapped in themselves and are willing to do what it takes to free it. Also to Linda Singlere who with her expertise and patience made this book better than it would have been without her.

Brian dedicates this book to dedicated people everywhere, as well as to people who feel they have burritos trapped in themselves and are willing to do whatever it takes to free them, but most importantly to his two puppies Bon Bon and Mo Mo, and to his wife Lynda Lynda.

# CONTENTS

# ACKNOWLEDGMENTS

We hereby would like to acknowledge everything.
Everything exists and we acknowledge it. You go, everything!

# INTRODUCTION

Hi! Welcome to a delightfully strange but eminently helpful book.

It's certainly a weird idea to base an entire business book on a Saturday Night Live sketch. But it's one of the most famous sketches ever from one of the funniest shows ever, and truth is comedy... only faster!

We think the "More Cowbell" sketch offers a ton of useful lessons — and some really ridiculous lessons as well.

Ridiculous can be good. And we wrote an entire chapter about redicularity. Isn't that ridiculous? No, we think it's good. Maybe we haven't gone far *enough*!

We hope you like it and stuff. Mostly "and stuff."

— Brian and Garrison


P.S. Get your three free Cowbell Principle BONUSES at:
http://thecowbellprinciple.com/bonuses

# 1. The Cowbell What?

**The Original "More Cowbell" Sketch**

"More Cowbell" is one of the most popular Saturday Night Live sketches of all time. It has permeated our culture. It's a meme. Most people have heard of it. If you haven't, hang on a second — we'll give you the link to the video and we'll go through the script momentarily. It's actually okay that you have not heard of it, and we don't mean to be offensive when we say... it's not your fault. You are most likely too old or too young to have been exposed to the really good things that life has to offer. The strategies in this book will work for anyone whether they have seen the sketch or not. So relax in your death bed, cancel your sponge bath, or cut your middle school math class and get ready to be free of your ignorance. And again, please don't take this the wrong way (your overwhelming ignorance and bad-birth-timing, I mean).

"More Cowbell" is hilarious. And as Brian accidentally discovered, it provides a profound analogy for self-discovery, self-improvement, mentoring, and teamwork. It offers clues about your life's purpose and how to be successful in life. Garrison's study of the sketch revealed parallels with top performers from almost every industry. He agreed with Brian that knowing what you love, knowing who values it, and handling people and situations while enjoying the moment could make anyone much more successful. They also agreed it would take a super-long sentence to convey that point.

Brian stumbled upon the sketch's practical applications while working on PowerPoint slides for his Social Media Marketing World 2014 breakout

1

session. He jokingly included a slide about "The Cowbell Principle," knowing that, to succeed at marketing, you need to give people something they have a fever for. Admittedly, he was working on little sleep and barely remembers creating the slide.

But it hit on some truths we've observed in recent years! Garrison (who has not slept since they stopped manufacturing Quaaludes in 1983) was instantly on board after seeing how Brian's analysis matched his own research. Determined but groggy, they moved forward with the project. They started by asking themselves a question that seemed at first glance almost too simple.

What's the biggest problem in communication? Too many companies we've worked with, too many consulting clients, brand managers, and ad agency account managers, have trouble putting themselves in their customers' shoes. Some of them aren't even aware they're not really achieving that. They don't realize there's a problem. Obviously you can't do the right thing if you don't have the vision to see what's wrong.

Too many startups never get off the ground because they're offering something nobody really wants. They're writing tweets and Facebook posts that nobody cares about. A student can almost never get a good grade if the professor does not believe the student understands the fundamental point of the subject. Leaders have no followers if they can't prove they know where they're going. Well, maybe Moses wandered a bit (40 years in a desert requires a lot of faith) but the Israelites believed in him because he and his boss "the G-O-D" had just magically drowned people who could build giant pyramids. Faith has a pretty good track record for creating more faith. So… that was one of Moses' cowbells.

The Cowbell Principle was originally just a funny slide to get people to think about serving other people. It got some laughs. But later when Brian went back and looked at what people tweeted during his presentation, he found that one of the biggest topics was the Cowbell Principle. Hmm.

Brian's an analytical nerd. (He has an Excel file analyzing all the jokes he has written.) He loves to dissect ideas, twist them, invert them, make analogies from them, always looking for an insight or metaphor that can lead to greater success. That means he can analyze a goofy comedy sketch and come up with something useful. So with that in mind, let's take a look at how the original sketch went down.

And if you want to watch it, Google "more cowbell hulu" or type this in: http://www.hulu.com/watch/536145

## Here's How It All Went Down…

Announcer: After a series of staggering defeats, Blue Öyster Cult assembled in the recording studio in late 1976 for a session with famed producer Bruce Dickinson. And, luckily for us, the cameras were rolling.

[Dissolve to recording studio]

Bruce Dickinson: Alright, guys, I think we're ready to lay this first track down. By the way, my name is Bruce Dickinson. Yes, the Bruce Dickinson. And I gotta tell you: fellas... you have got what appears to be a dynamite sound!

Eric Bloom: Coming from you, Bruce, that means a lot.

Buck Dharma: Yeah. I mean, you're Bruce Dickinson!

Joe: This is incredible!

Bobby: I can't believe Bruce Dickinson digs our sound!

Bruce Dickinson: Easy, guys... I put my pants on just like the rest of you — one leg at a time. Except, once my pants are on, I make gold records. [The group laughs.] Alright, here we go. "Fear... Don't Fear the Reaper" — take one. Roll it! [He exits into the control booth.]

Eric Bloom: Alright! One, two, three, four...

[The group starts the song: "All our times have come...Here but now they're gone..." — Bobby slaps the drums, Eric jams his guitar, and Gene bangs on a cowbell.]

Eric Bloom: [distracted by Gene banging the cowbell] Okay! Wait! Wait! Stop! [The group cuts off their instruments.] Um, Bruce, could you come in here for a minute, please?

Bruce Dickinson: [stepping out of the booth] That... that was gonna be a great track. Guys, what's the deal?

Eric Bloom: Uh, are you sure that was sounding okay?

Bruce Dickinson: I'll be honest... fellas, it was sounding great. But... I could've used a little more cowbell. So... let's take it again... and, Gene?

Gene Frenkle: Yeah?

Bruce Dickinson: Really explore the studio space this time.

Gene Frenkle: You got it, Bruce.

Bruce Dickinson: I mean, really... explore the space. I like what I'm hearing. Roll it.

[The group starts the song again, as Gene bangs more wildly onto the cowbell, gyrating his exposed belly. In the booth, (Christopher) Walken (who plays Bruce) is smiling to keep from laughing. Before the session is interrupted, Gene misses a beat on his cowbell.]

Eric Bloom: Okay, wait! Stop! Stop! Bruce, I'm sorry, could you come back in here, please?

Bruce Dickinson: [stepping out of the booth] Fellas... now, we just wasted two good tracks! This last one was even better than the first!

Eric Bloom: Well, it's just that I find Gene's cowbell playing distracting!

I don't know, if I'm the only one, I'll shut up.

Buck Dharma: Nah, it was pretty rough.

Gene Frenkle: You know, I could pull it back a little, if you'd like.

Bruce Dickinson: Not too much, though! I'm telling you, fellas — you're gonna want that cowbell on the track!

Gene Frenkle: You know what? It's fine. Let's just do the thing.

Bruce Dickinson: Okay, Roll it.

Eric Bloom: One, two, three, four...

[The band starts the song once more, with Gene banging the cowbell right next to Eric's ear until Eric pushes him, knocking over the microphone and causing Horatio Sanz (portraying bass player Joe Bouchard?) to fall.]

Eric Bloom: [stopping the song again, fighting Gene] COME ON, GENE!!

Gene Frenkle: NO, YOU COME ON!!

Bruce Dickinson: [running out of the booth again] Guys, y' know...that...that...it doesn't work for me. I gotta have more cowbell!

Joe: [grabs Gene's shirt] Don't blow this for us, Gene!

Bobby: [cracks up] Quit... quit being so selfish, Gene!

Gene Frenkle: Can I just say one thing?

Bruce Dickinson: Sure, baby! Just say it!

Gene Frenkle: I'm standing here, staring at rock legend Bruce Dickinson!

Bruce Dickinson: The cock of the walk, baby!

Gene Frenkle: And if Bruce Dickinson wants more cowbell, we should probably give him more cowbell!

Bruce Dickinson: Say it, baby!

Gene Frenkle: And, Bobby, you are right — I am being selfish. But the last time I checked, we don't have a whole lot of songs that feature the cowbell.

Bruce Dickinson: I gotta have more cowbell, baby!

Gene Frenkle: And I'd be doing myself a disservice — [begins to slightly laugh. Jimmy Fallon turns away and bites down on his drumstick to keep from laughing] and every member of this band, if I didn't perform the HELL out of this!

Bruce Dickinson: Guess what? I got a fever! And the only prescription... is more cowbell!

Gene Frenkle: Thank you, Bruce. But I think if... I think if I just leave... and maybe I'll come back later, and we can lay down the cowbell. [starts to leave the studio]

Bruce Dickinson: Aw, come on, baby...

Eric Bloom: Gene, wait! Why don't you lay down that cowbell right now. With us. Together.

[long pause while Gene looks around at the band]

Gene Frenkle: Do you mean that, Eric?

Eric Bloom: Oh, yeah.

Buck Dharma: He speaks for all of us.

Gene Frenkle: Thank you.

Bruce Dickinson: Babies… before we're done here… y'all be wearing gold-plated diapers.

Joe: [confused] What does that mean?

Bruce Dickinson: Never question Bruce Dickinson! Roll it! [exits back to booth]

[Gene picks up the fallen microphone and high-fives the drummer before getting into position.]

Eric Bloom: One, two, three, four…

[The band starts up again; this time Frenkle is playing the cowbell in tune with the band. Close-up on Gene as he bangs the cowbell to freeze-frame with graphic: "In Memoriam: Gene Frenkle: 1950-2000."]

[fade]

## Now Let's Break That Down

Here are the 10 lessons we see in the "More Cowbell" sketch. We find that these can be applied to both people and companies:

1.    DEMAND: You must find out what people have a fever for and then give them more of it. If it's going to qualify as a cowbell, it must be in demand. You have to care about what people want.

2.    MENTORSHIP: "Never question the Bruce Dickinson." It's important to have a mentor and objective ways to discover what people want. You have to find out what people really want, not just what you think they want.

3.    OPPOSITION: Not everybody's going to like your cowbell. Ignore their stupidfaces.

4.    TESTING: "You never know what's going to click." That's what Christopher Walken said in real life when he found out how popular the "More Cowbell" sketch was. You have to try a bunch of stuff to find the few great things.

5.    TEAMWORK: It's awesome to have a group of peers. You could have your own Blue Öyster Cult! (Except maybe your cult likes green clams…) Your cult will not always be right, and yet they'll still be awesome.

6.    HAPPINESS: Look at Gene. When you find your cowbell, you're

probably going to have a damn good time playing it.

7.   CREATIVITY: Sometimes you need to get creative and intuitive and "really explore the space."

8.   EXCESS: You can never have too much cowbell.

9.   FOOLISHNESS: Sometimes the dumbest idea is the best idea.

10.   PROFITS: Bruce said, "Before we're done here, y'all be wearin' gold-plated diapers." What does that even mean? We're going to tell you.

Each of those fundamentals has a chapter in this book, and each will deepen your ability to discover your cowbell(s), develop your cowbells, and use them to reach unprecedented levels of success in your life and career.

## Hey, Did You Get Your Free Cowbell Principle Bonuses?

As the owner of this book (even if you somehow got it for free) you are entitled to some awesome bonuses!

#1. The controversial chapter they made us take out! "You Can't Handle This Chapter: True Secrets of Success That Make People Uncomfortable" You may not want to read this one... it's very unconventional. But it's all so true that it's funny. And if you're the kind of person that just wishes people would level with you, you'll love it!

#2. The Superfun Cowbell Overview Webinar

#3. Mystery bonus!

To get them, go to http://thecowbellprinciple.com/bonuses and opt in!

# 2. Why Should I Care About What People Want?

One message of the Cowbell Principle is loud and clear: You have to find out what people have a fever for and then give them more of it. If it's really a cowbell, it's in demand. And that's why you can get paid to do it: People truly value your cowbell.

### What the Heck Is a Cowbell?

A cowbell is obviously something worn around a cow's neck that lets you know the cows are coming home, which, as we all know, does not happen very often. It makes sense that we would find another use for them. How someone suddenly thought "Hey, we should take the bell off that cow and use it in a song" can most likely be explained in two words: European drunkenness.

For the purpose of this book and based on the SNL sketch, the definition is as follows:

You have at least one cowbell — it's your unique, profitable talent or your company's unique offering. It's something people have a fever for. When you discover it and give those people a ton of it, you gain success and happiness for both yourself and others. It's a win-win.

A cowbell is simultaneously something you love doing and something other people really want as well (although, as we'll see, you still will have detractors, critics, and those who suffer from genius envy). A cowbell creates joy for you and other people. It makes them yell for more. They can't get enough.

Identifying and maximizing your cowbell will make you a happier person, a more valuable employee, and happier family member. But not everybody will like your cowbell. Some people (like the lead singer in the sketch) might even hate it. You can't even play a real cowbell everywhere all of the time or everyone will hate you. Get a life! A cowbell can be obnoxious in the wrong setting. It's like Tom Cruise: Producers and movie directors love him, but talk show hosts call security.

And Will Ferrell — is he crazy-funny all the time? Nope. If you listen to his interview with Marc Maron on the WTF podcast, you'll find out that he's like a lot of the comedians we know: Sometimes they're serious, sometimes quiet and sometimes profoundly humble. Good thing, too. We'd bet Will Ferrell's wife doesn't want him to act like "Frank the Tank" all the time.

Find out what people around you have a fever for and give them more of it. If you want to be in a different field, find out what people there have a fever for and give them more of it. We'll talk about research tools later. We'll also show you how to make sure people don't call you a tool as you pursue your goals.

How do you know when a person or a company has a cowbell? People are willing to part with hard-earned cash in return for it.

That doesn't mean it's easy to get paid or that people will pay you right away. Some people are lucky like that, but most aren't. You might have several talents and have to figure out which one to develop; or you might develop a lot of them and, through trial and error, figure out which one strikes the proper balance between your passion and what other people crave.

For example, your ability to navigate in a car without GPS might mean you have the kind of intuition it takes to change your direction in life. On the other hand, a unique gift for changing clothes while driving could get you arrested for drunk driving even though you totally pass the Breathalyzer.

## What Do You Do That Gets People Really Excited?

Not every talent is a cowbell, because not all talents are in demand. Your ability to play songs by rubbing wine glass rims probably isn't paying your mortgage. And that's not to take anything away from the few folks who do make an amazing living performing on 120 wine glasses in Las Vegas, if there are such people. Maybe you're a virtuoso on the triangle, the least-used percussion instrument in the history of music. All those triangle lessons — wasted! All that talent — useless! Just because you hit it with a stick does not make it a cowbell.

Sometimes a cowbell is more specific than a talent. Being analytical can be a talent, but maybe the particular way you use Excel pivot tables on research data is what academia pays you big bucks for. So certain types of nerdiness can be a cowbell. And, if that news wasn't uplifting enough for some of our readers, here's more good news: Nerds with cowbells have something most nerds don't have — girlfriends.

A cowbell might be best defined relative to the competition you face. Being bipedal may give you advantages over your pet cat, but your cat is not your main competition in life (we hope). Being seven feet tall is a big deal in college basketball but it's not enough in the NBA. The world is full of giant, untalented dufuses (dufi?), but if you're a seven-footer like Dirk Nowitzki who can make an absurd percentage of his fall-away jump shots, that's a goldang cowbell! To be fair, if you are extremely tall with zero basketball skills but you know how to act scary or menacingly weird, you might still end up in the movies.

Some niches are very personality based. If you're a realtor, a certain selling style may be more attractive to the ultra-rich who buy and sell mansions.  It takes more than big earrings and tall hair to close on a high-ticket house. You have to have a persona that is trusted by that type of customer. If you're in outside sales, your personality can be a huge asset to making an emotional connection with the customer. If your customers' buying process puts the decision in the hands of just one or two people, emotions can play a larger part in the buying decision, and your ability to persuade prospects emotionally becomes a very valuable cowbell.

Let's take a look at some more examples of cowbells so you can get an even better grasp on the concept.

Garrison honed a way to get laughs with great consistency. His cowbell is, in part, being hilarious. "My cowbell is that I'm really good in front of a live audience," he explains. "Because of that I honed being entertaining and delivering a live message with great content. A lot of people tell me I am very good and they enjoyed my keynote. But at least five to six times a year, someone tells me I really have a gift. I'll hear, 'I've seen a lot of speakers but you have a true gift.'"

For Brian, implementation is a strong suit. As he puts it, "My cowbell is getting things done. I have the skill of a CEO and a writer and speaker… but my cowbell doesn't have to be exercised in the writing field. If I ran a dude ranch, I'd make whatever is supposed to happen on a dude ranch happen. I'd learn; I'd make it happen; and then, over time, I'd turn it into one of the best dude ranches a dude has ever seen. I am implementation-oriented and focused. If I don't know how to do something, I learn how and I get it done. I can move on to something else." Although he loves comedy, he doesn't identify it as his main moneymaker. It's more of a differentiating secondary cowbell (discussed later in this chapter). "Comedy is really just a tactic I use to create things that people love and to get them to enjoy what I'm teaching. It helps differentiate my style from others, as well," he notes.

Some of the cowbells in stories throughout the book:

• A speaker whose cowbell is to inform and entertain — specifically by modeling his behavior on how rock stars perform.
• A startup entrepreneur whose cowbell is to focus in with OCD-like, laser-level obliviousness to solve problems.
• A PR professional whose company's cowbell is to address the biggest PR problem that PR itself has.
• A tall musician chick who knows how to ask with vulnerability.
• An author and speaker whose cowbells are to forecast trends, simplify complex topics, and draw out people's stories by listening.

We want to emphasize that although many of the stories in this book come from entrepreneurs, freelancers, or artists, by no means does that mean you can't have a cowbell or two as a COO or accountant or IT person. Some of the most successful people on earth have unsexy jobs where their cowbell makes them fantastic. Keep in mind that in the "More Cowbell" sketch, it's the normally insignificant cowbell that is in demand. The entrepreneurial or creative types whose stories we feature in chapters to come are simply the people we had access to. And these more extreme examples (of the crazy individualism of artists) make the point easier to see. As this book goes out and people of all types read it, we hope you'll send us your cowbell story so we can do a second edition with a more diverse set of stories.

**Real-World Examples Of Cowbells**
• If you're more empathetic than most, that can help you as a doctor, therapist, parent, or mid-level manager. Maybe you're a volunteer counselor at your church.
• If you have exceptional confidence, vision, or standards, those things can help you be a more effective leader.
• If you're hilarious and a clear communicator, like Garrison, you can get paid very well to keynote more than 100 times a year.
• If you're good at learning and systematizing, like Brian, you can get paid to teach or train or keynote (especially if you're also entertaining).
• If you love to bring people together for mutual benefit like Derek

Coburn, you'll always have a strong network, which brings you opportunities and magnifies them.

## Is There Icing on Your Cake?

A cowbell is like the icing on a cake.

What do people think about cake with no icing? It's not that exciting. You're not going to compulsively choose it and eat it. A cake without icing is just a giant muffin!

Employees with no icing don't stand out. They don't have an advantage. They can be fired and easily replaced. Companies can lack icing, too. They're mediocre and dull and have no differentiation from other companies. They can have lower-than-average customer loyalty. Who wants a big plain muffin when they can have cake? I am not dishonoring muffins, just making a point. Imagine the guests at your birthday party walk out singing "Happy Birthday to You" while holding a thick disk of bald bread with burning candles jammed in it. What do you have when you take the icing away from a cake? Muffin! Absolutely muffin!

But eating only icing will make you sick. No matter what your cowbell is, you'll come across lots of boring, everyday tasks you have to do, unless you are one of the lucky few who can give all their non-cowbell responsibilities to assistants. That's the basic premise of the book The 4-Hour Work Week: outsource everything you're not uniquely great at. But most of us who have attempted to work for only four hours a week went out of business or got fired. Ironically, when you're then forced to live on welfare, you really can work just four hours a week, recycling all your beer cans!

All kidding aside, for those who have the opportunity, there is real merit to the strategy: specialize and rely on other specialists. But not all of us have that option. In fact, many of us can't even think of outsourcing the muffin stuff because we have yet to identify our icing.

Exactly what is your cake and what is your icing? Make a list with two columns. The first column is cake: things you have to do that a lot of other people could do. The second column is icing: the unique things you do that are irreplaceable.

Don't devalue those mundane tasks just because your icing column seems so awesome. That naked, doughy gluten glob eventually gets baked into the sweet success that is your cowbell. We suspect everyone has plenty of stuff to list in that cake column… but if you don't have any icing, you'd better make some!

## Wow, I Didn't Know I Had a Cowbell

We learned something really interesting about cowbells by asking people to submit stories of their own cowbell: Some people have a cowbell but don't realize it. Some people are fortunate that things in their psyche or life are working for them, regardless of their awareness. They really don't know why they've succeeded. Maybe they think it's luck. Luck is what happens to people who are always prepared to be good. So, more often than not, they are.

Some people, like Jessie Shternshus (whose story is in the Confidence chapter), have never struggled with finding or developing a cowbell. They found their cowbell early in life and have stuck with it.

## Can You Have More Than One Cowbell?

Yes.

And your cowbell can change with the situation. Rajiv's story later in this chapter is a great example of that.

## Some Hobbies Could Be Cowbells

You don't have to get paid to do your cowbell right now. You can develop your talents and get paid later.

Brian loved speaking to audiences and did so for 11 years before anybody paid him for it. In fact, some people have a cowbell where they don't get paid so they have more freedom and choice and purity. Brian's wife, for example, didn't enjoy acting in Hollywood but loves community theater. She also enjoys it now when Brian is paid to speak so he can have the freedom to pay the bills. But the attempt to retroactively collect on those 11 years of past engagements was an odd choice!

Musical talent plus practice can make you a professional musician. Lynda enjoyed Brian's guitar playing, and a song he wrote her was a catalyst to their relationship. But Brian was not interested in the lifestyle of the struggling musician. He believes the world already has plenty of talented poor people and does not visualize himself as one of them. Brian loves stand-up comedy but some of his jokes don't fit in a corporate setting, so he does stand-up for free at open mics, or he gets paid $20, maybe. He doesn't pursue club-style comedy gigs. He's been paid $1,500 to do social media comedy and $7,500 to keynote, but he can only play some of his humor cowbell at those keynotes. Corporate event organizers often frown upon certain elements of comedy; in fact, we scrapped the final line of this paragraph out of respect for the many super-stiff, humorless wretches who might have been offended by it.

Your cowbell hobbies can save your keister, too. Brian walked onstage to do his keynote for NBC, and despite extensive planning and practice with the tech crew, Brian's presentation didn't come up on the screen for three minutes. During that time he tap-danced… in the form of doing some of his clean, corporate-ready stand-up jokes. Without all those nights doing stand-up for free at open mics, he wouldn't have been ready. Instead, he overcame a horrible situation and looked even more professional for it.

Of course, success here depends on the hobby… Had he started making model airplanes for three minutes, it might have been slightly less impressive!

## Cowbells vs. Bagpipes

Pablo Picasso said, "The meaning of life is to find your gift. The purpose of life is to give it away."

The Cowbell Principle is not "Follow your joy and the money will follow." Maybe you love painting watercolors but nobody likes your watercolor paintings. That's not a cowbell.

There may be something you love to do that you hope is your cowbell, but no one else cares about it. Or, worse yet, maybe they actively dislike you doing it. ("Oh man, Dad is playing bass in the basement again?! Is he never going to realize he sucks?") Many people have followed their joy right into the unemployment line. You have to bring joy to others for it to be a truly cowbellian experience.   Additionally, most people who do things in basements are not that great and frequently are, or should be, arrested.

If no one has a fever for it, it's not a cowbell.

In fact, we'll call it something else: bagpipes. In real life, a bagpipe is something you love to play but a lot of other people find annoying.

It doesn't matter if you have a gift or passion, if it's not valuable to other people. That's the difference between a cowbell and a bagpipe. Your cowbell is the biggest talent you have that other people have a fever for. Bagpipes are not cowbells.

A note to the Scottish: We think bagpipes are awesome. Brian almost bought some once. He would love to play outlawed tunes on outlawed pipes. But most people aren't big fans. Except when the bagpipes are part of an AC/DC song. In which case, people agree: THEY EFFING ROCK.

For the most part, people are not going around yelling, "More bagpipes!" They're not thinking, "Dang, I just don't have enough bagpipe in my life." No, they hear bagpipes and they think, "Oh, that's interesting," and then within a minute or two they're wondering, "How can I get away from these bagpipes?" Maybe you've noticed that bagpipe players always walk as they play — because everyone else is walking away from them, creating a strange slow-motion Celtic chase scene.

Garrison has a very different view of the bagpipes but overall agrees with Brian: "Sales for bagpipe recordings are, well, nonexistent. Every song ever played on the bagpipes reminds me of why the Scottish are so cranky. Their contributions historically are golf, whiskey, bad music, bad food, and man-skirts — which, as we know, all lead to alcoholism. I am not criticizing the bagpipes or Scotland (okay, I very much just did and I apologize). I'm just making a point. Some things are not in demand even though we enjoy them."

Sometimes parents screw up their kids by buying them bagpipes. What we mean by that is, they push their kids toward one career path or another. But as Chinese wise guy Chin-Ning Chu said, "A successful life is one that is lived through understanding and pursuing one's own path, not chasing after the dreams of others." Don't think that quote makes us really wise and cultured. We just found it on the Internet.

If you're doing something that's not your cowbell, we're not going to condemn you. It's okay to have a hobby that's just for you. But you should know what your cowbell is and do that too. Unfortunately, many people aren't pursuing or playing their cowbells. We haven't always either. Bagpipes can easily distract.

You have to be honest with yourself about specific bagpipe activities. Your dreams of professional skateboarding will not take you very far at age 41. You'll just be that long-haired guy in the airport wearing Vans, board under your arm, in either really long short pants or really short long pants, and using reading glasses to text.

Video games also are fun and take your mind off of stressful things like reality. But Call of Duty is not your calling. It's a bagpipe.

What both of these activities have in common is they require that your mom consistently pays your rent. And Bruce Dickinson does not want you to live that way.

On a day-to-day basis, we all have to do many things we're not passionate about. That's the cake. For example, Brian's not a big fan of sleep. Of course, no one would consider sleep a cowbell... except maybe Snow White.

Rarity does not a cowbell make. That short, Yoda-style sentence is very important to understand as you move through the chapters of this book. Rare does not always equal valuable, as any viewer of the show Pawn Stars has learned. Sometimes the reason something is the only one in existence is because nobody wanted a second one. A cowbell has to be in demand; it must be wanted; it needs to give people a "fever for more."

Ultimately, success means getting clearer and clearer about what your cowbell is and trying to outsource your cake. And hey, one person's cake is another person's icing. You'll do even better if you're outsourcing your cake to someone whose cowbell is your cake. Confused yet? Good.

Here's a practical example. Brian detests accounting and billing, so he has someone else do that. Garrison does the same. And of course, some people — accountants — love that. They have their own conferences and stuff where their parties look almost as fun as anyone else's most boring workday. Surrendering those responsibilities means more time to play your cowbell. Brian gives the taxes to tax preparers who are exceptionally good at lowering his tax liabilities — and that's their cowbell. Garrison turns his taxes over to Courtney, his office manager, who is very good at lowering his stress.

Liability and stress? Cake, cake, cake to Brian and Garrison. Too much cake leaves no room for icing! It's important to create space in your life for the sweet taste of success.

Apart from bagpipes, there's another class of things called "killer skills" that are not nearly as awesome as they sound. They're not killer as in, "killer half pipe, dude!" or "those Wayfarer sunglasses are too killer!" No, it's not the 1980s version of the term. They're killer in that they kill your spirit. Ouch!

Killer skills are things you've learned to do that make you money, but they're not a passion; in fact, they're the opposite of a passion and they are slowly killing you. They're tough to let go of if they're earning you money, especially if you're really afraid of going bankrupt and being homeless. So it's easy to get trapped in those activities because you think that kind of misery is just "responsible." Maybe being without a home is a possibility, but most of us would not be out in the street; we'd just be stuck with people we'd rather avoid. Moving in with your parents (no offense to those of you who never left) or moving in with the guy from college you didn't want to hang out with until he bought a three-bedroom townhouse (and then remembering after a week exactly why he'll always be looking for a new roommate) — these are all very achievable levels of homelessness. Worrying about these scenarios keeps us in the living death of a killer skill.

"We must be willing to let go of the life we planned so as to have the life that is waiting for us." — Joseph Campbell

Even if you're nowhere close to being homeless, it's possible to think you are. Fear has penned in a whole bunch of us, so we devote a section to that later in the Opposition chapter.

Wondering if the thing you think is your cowbell might instead be a bagpipe? Not everyone has to like your cowbell. It could be an obscure interest or hobby, like boxing with midgets or collecting art made exclusively from sausage casing. It's only a bagpipe if almost everybody hates it and you can't get paid for it. Not everybody likes Night Ranger or Tesla, but they still make a living as musicians. Very few people like croquet as a spectator sport because it lacks a certain…well… everything. And yet, some people really love it — especially for the lawn party held at each match. Sure, those people are often arrested for drunk driving, but they have a fever for being intoxicated and watching people hit balls through hoops. You don't have to have a big market to have a valuable and loyal market. In fact, smaller markets can be easier to dominate because the competition is often mediocre.

Here's an example of a cowbell that's a bagpipe to many people: Brian feels ambivalent about puns but his brain produces a punishing amount of them. When he does stand-up, he constantly tests jokes and listens for the response. Hipsters tell him with their groans that his puns are bagpipes. But at his keynote for Life Technologies, the audience of scientists-turned-marketers loved the custom puns he wrote for them about their niche. They laughed harder at the puns than at anything else. He was so shocked that he committed a big stand-up comedy error: He told them they weren't supposed to laugh at puns so much. They quieted down, but as he told more, they returned to their crazy levels of laughter. Apparently, smart people like puns. (Some interesting research shows that people who like puns are more psychologically secure, which explains why the hip young folks in downtown Charleston don't like Brian's puns; they're both insecure and dumb! That theory certainly makes him feel better. Don't tell them he said this.) In this case, Brian's puns are bagpipes for most people but a cowbell for others!

Garrison, who is mercifully less punny (and thinks that makes him real cool), speaks in Europe sometimes, where he pulls out jokes that poke fun at American culture and stereotypes. The bits don't work in the U.S. (trust us on that). But, in a ballroom full of Brits and Germans, talking about how Americans need more of the world's energy resources because our giant SUVs burn lots of petrol as we take our big fat families to Burger King just kills. They laugh and applaud like crazy. The seven Americans in the front row think Garrison's traitor and have reported him to Homeland Security, but Hans from Munich is the guy who's paying him. Hans is the Bruce Dickinson who wants more of what separates Garrison from other American business speakers who present overseas. So Garrison gets the gold-plated diapers.

Just because some people don't enjoy something you love now does not mean you can't turn it into a cowbell. Brian uses a story from his life to show how, with determination and effort, you can turn a weakness that you have a fondness for into a moneymaker — even though for him the process took about 11 years.

## How Brian Turned Something He Was Horrible At Into One Of His Biggest Cowbells

If you look at yourself and you don't see the talent you want to have yet, that's not necessarily the end of the story. It doesn't mean you can't learn to do that thing. Brian, who has always loved learning and teaching, spent a lot of time trying to expand his abilities to help others. However, social phobia and shyness prevented him from being able to take his expertise and help people. He wanted to speak to a ton of people but didn't know if they'd want him to!

After getting a master's degree and learning a lot about Eastern and Western medicine, Brian taught a medical terminology class. Surprisingly, he had the students rolling in the aisles. Other teachers and students wondered what was going on in that class — what was the topic? Medical terminology?! But that's tremendously boring! Why are they laughing so much?

Somehow Brian had become funny. Later, looking back at a fake school newspaper he'd written in sixth grade, he realized he'd always had his own brand of humor, but being socially phobic, he had little opportunity for that to come out.

That teaching experience gave him the guts to try pure stand-up comedy. Eventually, he came to believe that comedy open mics are like the boot camp of speaking. It's a rough situation. No one knows you, and they want to laugh immediately. "Who's this guy?" When you're new, you have no proven material. That's the worst it ever gets. It can only get better.

Before going on stage, he read 11 books about stand-up and wrote 100 pages of material. A self-admitted nerd, he recorded every set, created an Excel document to track which jokes they laughed at, and rated that level of laughter 1 through 10, an entry for every night he performed. He found that only about 5% of what he wrote was funny. Other famous comedians have mentioned a similar percentage, especially at the start of a career. That means you fail 95% of the time! Failure is a big part of developing a cowbell, especially if it's new to you.

From his scholastic teaching pursuits, Brian learned a lot about digital marketing. He started down the path of "thought leadership" by blogging a lot about Google advertising. And after about three years of speaking at conferences and working with his Bruce Dickinson of speaking (Garrison Wynn), he started earning a real living. It took years, but it was worth it.

He worked hard enough and long enough to be able to speak in a way that people enjoyed and valued. Once Brian Carter's speeches were a bagpipe. But sometimes you can turn bagpipes into cowbells.

If you went back and looked at who Brian was at age 6 or 16, there's no way you would say he could be where he is. He took a serious weakness and turned it into a cowbell. And you can, too, if you're willing to work.

The easier path, though — and easier isn't a bad thing — is to go with the things you're already strong at. From experience, Brian advises doing that first and primarily. For instance, while working on his speaking skills, Brian was also utilizing these cowbells:

- Data analysis to find tactics that yield greater results
- Writing prolifically (blogs and books)
- Implementing often and quickly

## Does That Have to Be My Cowbell, Really?

Speaking might not have been Brian's natural forte, but he knew what was: writing.

He had read and written a ton all his life. He spent much of his socially phobic time having a blast reading Star Trek novels and listening to Yes and Asia. He even started to write some of his own sci-fi. All of this kept him from getting dates, because it was the 80's. In college, his major required that he write a lot of papers and learn academic research standards. When he earned his master's degree, he helped design graduate-level courses, wrote hundreds of online articles, and wrote his first book. He wrote 82 blog posts about AdWords from 2007 to 2010. Later he wrote three more books.

Writing is his cowbell. He writes well. He writes clearly. He churns out a lot of good writing in a tenth of the time it takes most people.

But, you know what? He genuinely wishes it wasn't his cowbell. Speaking is more glamorous. Writing is a weird, nerdy thing people do alone in their rooms. And most people don't even like reading. Most bestselling business books don't get finished by the people who buy them. Still, writing a book boosts your profile and credibility. You get **author**ity from being an author.

Still, Brian admits he loves reading, because it improves your life and gives you more opportunities. He's also taking a screenwriting class. Why? He wants to learn to do it. Most people don't pay to learn to write better. That's just more evidence writing is one of his passions.

Your cowbell is something you love to do, something you are or could be really, really good at, and that people have a fever for.

## Let Go of Your Bagpipes

One of the biggest obstacles to getting anywhere with a cowbell is when you're attached to a bagpipe that will never be your cowbell. I really hope you're not in that situation.

Sometimes we just love something so much that we can't see it's dragging us down. So it's time you (the reader) and we (Brian and Garrison) get super honest.

## Self-Honesty As A Personal Success Tool

Questions to ask yourself:

1.     Are you willing to consider that something you strongly believe is not even close to being true?
2.     Is it possible that one of the reasons your perceived cowbell is a total bagpipe is because you are delusional about your proficiency?
3.     Are you attached to the bagpipe because it allows you to avoid your true cowbell, which would cause you see what your real talent and abilities are?
4.     Do you think the talents and abilities you possess are not impressive enough to the people whose opinions you truly value?
5.     Is it possible that you are living your life through the filter of someone else?
6.     Could you, in fact, be living someone else's dreams?

Sometimes we grow up with a vision of what we truly want in our head and our heart, only to find out later that the vision had been planted there by someone else — possibly aliens, but most likely our parents and relatives. It was your father who wanted to be a lawyer, not you. It was your Uncle Karen who wanted to be a Dolly Parton impersonator, not you. It was your mother who wanted to be cremated and have her ashes spread over Tom Selleck, not you. If you tried to be everything others wanted you to be, you'd be a cremated Dolly Parton–impersonating lawyer. The truth is other people's dreams cannot create your future.

But look at Earl Boykins, who at 5'5" had a great NBA career. He could still leap, he was quick and he practiced his shot until it he was a sharpshooter. You may have enough gifts to pull off your dream, even if you don't have one of the most obvious gifts people have in that career.

Still, when you're learning, you may become discouraged and wonder if you're on the wrong track. Not sure if something is your cowbell? Try giving it up for six months and see how you feel. If you're okay, maybe it was never meant to be your cowbell.

You also want to try new things, because your cowbell might be something you've never done!

List four or five things you haven't done that you'd like to.

**Examples:**
Have lunch with Morgan Freeman in a hot air balloon.
Open a Swiss cheese pizza parlor.
Invest in pig futures. (Even though, pigs don't have much of a future; their destiny is to be pork.)
Touch Donald Trump's hair (or whatever that is on his head).

**Okay, a real list of examples:**
Start a small business that you love.
Take your family on that trip you've always talked about.
Take lessons or get coaching in those areas where you know you have talent.
Learn a foreign language (hopefully one that the foreigners in your life actually speak).
Spend some money on yourself.

Try one possible cowbell out per week for a while. If no one is depending on you like a spouse or child, you have more freedom to try things. But needing to make money can also be a big motivator. (We'll talk about that in the Profits chapter.) Nobody, including you, knows how successful your cowbell could be.

Even highly successful people play the bagpipes occasionally. Brian was listening to a live recording of U2 singing "I Still Haven't Found What I'm Looking For" in Italy; at the beginning of the song, after announcing they were recording a DVD (to which the crowd really didn't react that strongly), Bono for some reason started to ramble about how Italy invented the movies because stained-glass windows were the first cinema... the crowd was relatively quiet until he began to sing.

A rock star talking too long before a song is a bagpipe. One of the big keys to success is to do very little of what you clearly don't do well.

## Cowbells vs. Purple Cows

It would have been impossible to write this book without being made aware of Seth Godin's book *Purple Cow*. One of our earliest sounding boards for the idea pointed out that he had already done "a cow thing."

The Cowbell Principle is not the same concept. It actually raises the bar on the Purple Cow.

First, we disagree with the popular trend among gurus, which Godin puts forth in Purple Cow, to argue that advertising doesn't work anymore and that things only spread by word of mouth. This is complete and udder bullshit. (That was an awesome pun, and impossible for Brian to resist.) Organizations spend big money on advertisements and have learned that the opposite is true.

As a former corporate guy with Fortune 500 and midsize companies, Garrison witnessed the power of advertising. The results were measurable and could even be tracked to the specific source of marketing that created them. Currently, his own company's ads generate business every week. He characterizes marketing, social media, and advertising as word of mouth on steroids.

Brian has lived and breathed digital marketing and advertising for the last 15 years and has encountered some weird theories such as "conversations are more important than selling" or "social media ROI can't be measured." But his experience and his customers' results tell us those things aren't true.

The main concept of Godin's book is that your business must be remarkable. But we feel that uniqueness isn't enough. If you have a remarkably unique company that doesn't do anything useful, who cares? Only the media, perhaps. If you have a remarkably unique company created by passionless people who simply followed a process, how are you going to connect emotionally with your customers? At worst, a Purple Cow is flashy Dennis Rodman wearing earrings and marrying himself and eating meals with communist dictators, but without his amazing defensive abilities — which, ahem, is what he actually got paid for. So, while Purple Cow has some good points, let's be clear that it's not at all what we are talking about in this book.

Jay Baer's book *Youtility* talks about the importance of a business being useful to the customer. We think both successful people and companies must first be useful. You must solve customers' problems. Give Rodman the ability to get 20 to 30 rebounds in a playoff game and then he's more than just a weirdo.

The Cowbell Principle consists of 10 different things, which we think makes it a more credible system.

The main components of the Cowbell Principle are —

• Fever for the cowbell: People actually want it.

- Bruce Dickinson: Mentorship, having support from the people in power, and having a compass that points you in the right direction.
- Gene playing the hell out of that cowbell: Happiness, excessiveness, enthusiasm, and not being afraid to look foolish.
- Community: Fitting into your team in a constructive way and making a contribution.

Uniqueness in many cases can be one of the least important things. Was Gene Frenkle the only cowbell player in the world? No, but he was in the right community (Blue Öyster Cult), he had passion, and he had the support of the guy who was the ultimate decision maker.

Was Dennis Rodman the only player the Bulls could have acquired to ensure they won a championship? No, and many teams would have had big problems with him, because of his often weird and rebellious behavior. But because of Phil Jackson's genius management skills (his cowbell), Rodman had a huge impact. In that case, Phil Jackson played the Bruce Dickinson part. And Rodman himself is proof that sometimes a cowbell is more than just being unique. The way uniqueness fits into the Cowbell Principle is this: Your cowbell is a complex thing that leverages all 10 fundamentals in a unique way.

When it comes down to it, the biggest similarity this book has to Purple Cow is that the word "cow" is involved. So don't have a cow, man.

## How to Be Irreplaceable

The job with the greatest security is the one that only you can do.

No one can replace Oprah — not exactly. You can do something similar and be Ellen or Rosie, both of whom have slightly different audiences. Conan, Leno, Letterman, Kimmel, and Fallon all do similar things but have very different audiences, with Kimmel's audience seeming slightly more intoxicated than the others.

There's always more room for someone who is unique and has value. Value, like beauty, is in the eye of the beholder. What we value can change as well. So it's important to recheck the values of the people you want to influence.

It's your job to do what you love but also to make sure it helps somebody. The TV hosts mentioned above discovered their cowbell and positioned themselves to play it where people could enjoy it. Then they each continued to develop their cowbell while getting paid for it. Here's what we think their cowbells are:

Leno: Quick, funny lines and banter during guest interviews, more like

Johnny Carson (whom he replaced) than the others.

Letterman: Irreverent enough to attract a younger crowd, corny enough for average viewers, and not afraid to rock the boat of the talk show world.

Fallon: Extreme likeability, clear respect for his guests, and variety-show talent, all of which make up for the fact he was never a professional stand-up comedian.

Kimmel: Makes you feel that even if you're drunk or have had run-ins with the law, you are still welcome; connects well to viewers who might not watch other talk shows (or even own a TV).

What they all have in common is we seem to feel they should be TV talk show hosts.

Coco Chanel once said (between perfume spritzes), "In order to be irreplaceable, one must always be unique." Coco was all about style. She knew that the bottle you put a fragrance in had a lot to do with how many you sold. She understood a new fragrance had to have a different-looking container and an ad campaign that separated it from the last thing she introduced.

David Bowie is a great example of someone who reinvented himself many times. Who else could be David Bowie but David Bowie? Some musicians have one or two similarities to Bowie, but no one completely matches his creative diversity and changeability. Though influenced by Marc Bolan of T. Rex, Bowie cut his own path and took it to a higher level. Where Bolan experimented with femininity, Bowie took it further in the early 1970s in a way that made people take note. As Garrison's dad commented upon first seeing Bowie on TV, "A woman that ugly could have never gotten a record deal."

## People Gotta Want It

It's not enough to be unique. You have to be in demand and valuable enough to get paid.

Two things can keep a hobby from becoming something more:

1.  You don't have enough passion to do it 40 or more hours a week.
2.  No one would pay you to do it, so you don't have 40 spare hours to spend on it.

Your hobby may be unique, but if there's no demand for it, it has no value for others. It might even disturb some people that you want to do it. Tons of people can do "stupid human tricks" that are interesting but useless. We just watched a video where a boy broke the world record for the highest musical pitch ever whistled. So what? Who would pay for that? The reality is that dogs would not show up for this guy — and even if they did, dogs rarely have money. It didn't even sound entertaining. Most world records are pointless. The greatest achievement of the guy with the world's longest fingernails is pretty much just being gross!

If you want to make money, uniqueness isn't enough. Everyone has a unique fingerprint but no one is trying to buy your fingerprint. (If they are, you should be suspicious.) You must be unique but also uniquely valuable.

Brian discovered in his 20s that when you truly help another person at a deep or transformative level — if you can change or perhaps even help save a person's life — you find a satisfaction and meaning unparalleled in life. We are made to help each other, and that's why it feels so good. Brian never experienced that kind of contentment — the feeling that he was okay and in the right place — from anything else. Not from eating an expensive meal. Not from sex. Not from tons of retweets on a blog post. Not from writing a weird book based on a ridiculous Saturday Night Live sketch.

Garrison discovered in his 20s that he would wait until his 30s to actually do anything significant. But in his 30s he too found that helping others was what made life better for everyone. And it was why humans survived as a species when we were otherwise not so well equipped. We helped each other. We depended on each other. You could not single us out like water buffalo and take us out one by one. We would come back and gang up on you. A mother lion or gorilla might protect its young briefly, but we humans were consistently willing to die for one another for the survival of future generations. We might not have had speed, strength, toughness, or what might be perceived as common sense or instinct by other animals, but we just kind of refused to be extinct. We took advantage of our brain and our ability to see the big picture and literally removed ourselves from the food chain. That's the human race's cowbell. The other animals can't wipe us out. If we go extinct, we'll do it ourselves and take everything with us! Okay, that's dramatic. The point is that all humans are naturally born to succeed, though we are different and have varied talents.

True to form, we want to help you discover your talent.

## Why People Don't Care, Even When They Know You Care

The old cautionary quote for know-it-alls is that "People don't care how much you know until they know how much you care." It's true. But it's only two-thirds of the equation.

People have recently tried to apply this quote to business. It sounds like this: "Customers don't care how much you know until they know how much you care."

FALSE! This quote originally was used for people trying to pass on knowledge one-on-one, not for companies. Companies are different. This quote needs to evolve, because the truth is that your customers don't care how much you care if you can't solve their problem. A customer is by definition someone who is buying or has bought something. If you were shopping for cars and the very caring car salesman (this is a fictional example) tries to sell you a nice jacket and some shoes, what would you think? Probably "I don't care how much he cares" and "I am never shopping for a car at Macy's again!"

People first have to want what you have, and then caring helps you get them to pay you for it instead of someone else.

Caring about people doesn't matter much if you can't improve their lives. Brian's grandma cares about him but she can't help him with his taxes and she hasn't programmed a helpful social media tool. Thus, his grandma can't help him with his taxes or manage a ton of social media. So when Brian's facing those problems, his grandma caring about him is nice but irrelevant.

Caring is the foundation of mankind's survival. But if you clearly are not even trying to solve the right problems, people won't care enough to buy from you.

**To Serve Humans**

Extrta points for you if you get that Twilight Zone reference. It's here in response to the question that drives this little section of the book: "Why do you do what you do?"

The best answer is "I enjoy it and it helps people." For some, family members are the only important people to help. It's enough that their paycheck helps their family. Other people want more than money from their work; they want meaning. Still others don't have family and can therefore devote more hours to work or to community building. A few others want world domination, but luckily most of those people still live with their moms, usually in the attic or basement.

Everybody has to help somebody. You can get away with only so much enjoyment that benefits you and you alone — and these solo activities can even become self-destructive. When helping others is fundamental to your mission, it keeps you from becoming too self-indulgent. If you strive to create success for those around you as you try to achieve your own goals, your self-absorption can be kept to a livable minimum.

Ultimately, it's not all about you. Personal passion must be part of why you do what you do, but it also needs to be "other focused." A cowbell comes from a desire to serve in a unique way. If it doesn't help other people, it isn't a cowbell. Years ago, Garrison knew a woman who could smoke a cigarette and chew gum at the same time. Though her breath was uniquely confusing, it did not help others. Ashtray-scented Bazooka breath does not benefit anyone, regardless of the passion with which it's delivered.

If you're very self-centered, you might only accept the idea of helping other people as something you have to do to get what you want. You check it off the list, and that's enough.

But people really shine when they love the people who have a fever for their cowbell.

Brian and his wife recently went out to a downtown Charleston restaurant. They watched with amusement as one tie-dyed, dreadlocked man set up speakers and a keyboard on the patio, and then proceeded to record and play back in a loop a bass line, a reggae backing guitar… then he soloed over it, then sang over it, then recorded a backing vocal and sang over that. Brian joked to his wife, "In this economy, even entertainers are having to wear two and three hats." Maybe the restaurant hired a multiple-personality musician because he could do the whole-band himself and they only had to pay him solo-performer money.

It's a downsize-and-make-do mindset that has persisted from the troubled economy of 2008. And it means one good thing- that if you have a passion for what you do, and other people will pay you for it, and you don't mind doing a few associated things without letting them become soul-quashing killer skills, you earn yourself some pretty tight job security.

Garrison was being checked into a very small airport near a remote resort by a young lady wearing a reflective yellow vest, shorts, and a shoulder radio. She put the luggage on the conveyer and then walked through a door behind the check-in counter. As he was boarding the plane, he saw the woman putting bags into the cargo hold. He thought to himself, "This 21-year-old woman does almost everything at this airport!" As the 10-passenger plane began to taxi, Garrison, in the first passenger seat right behind the pilot, could see through the front windshield the same woman guiding the plane toward the runway.

Garrison asked the copilot, "Who is that?"

"That's Morgan, the airport girl."

"Are there any other employees at this airport?" Garrison asked.

"Not since they hired Morgan."

Fewer people are employed and they're doing more work. Many always feel behind. More and more are available via email or social media outside the regular 9 to 5.

It's a tough economy. It's never been more important for you to have a personal competitive advantage in your career. That advantage gives you some job security and will help secure your next job. Morgan the airport girl seemed to be a jack of all trades by way of attrition. Companies run lean these days and if you don't have a cowbell but you're a hard worker, you may end up like Morgan.

It's as if you're either constantly improving (and controlling your fate) or trapped doing the work of the people who were let go.

Our fears are not of not surviving, but of mediocrity and powerlessness. We want to be empowered to win. We want to stay ahead. That's how we stay above water and surf the big waves.

In our opinion, if you're just keeping up, you're actually falling behind. As Garrison often says, treading water is definably not swimming; it's simply controlled drowning.

## How Playing Your Cowbell Could Make Billions of People Want You

So maybe your cowbell won't be desired by billions of people — maybe just the people you want to directly affect to achieve your goal ... or maybe just your boss (although being desired by your boss sounds a bit icky) ... or your parents or your dog. Frankly, if you can't get your dog to want you, it might just be time to stash some bacon in your pants.

The point is this: When you're playing your cowbell with passion, your efforts will create influence. If you choose to not to develop your advantages, you run the risk of being mired in mediocrity.

Brian is an avid fan of indie rock and obscure bands. Some bands that are unknown on radio and TV still have a remarkable online followings. For example, The Joy Formidable, a bombastic three-piece from Wales, has more than 140,000 Facebook fans. But odds are you've never heard of them.

Comedian Paul F. Thompkins has a podcast and cult following all over the country. He's toured theaters for years with the arrangement that if his fans can get 150 people to buy tickets, he will come and perform for them.

This is microfame. But for the artists, there's nothing micro about it. Making enough money to live and getting to perform their art is more than enough success for them.

Sure, some of us want U2-level success. But not many can achieve that. For example, the average rock band member makes just $50-100 per show. But if your primary goal is to play for audiences, that may be all you need.

When you find the thing you offer that people have a fever for and give them a ton of it, they pay attention to you, they love you, and you have personally meaningful success.

If you haven't seen Amanda Palmer's TED Talk, check it out. She asks people for help or money, and she's successful because of her cowbell of being extremely vulnerable. A combination of street performing, crowd surfing, and rock band touring led to one of the most successful Kickstarter campaigns ever. Her goal was $100,000. She received funding from 24,000 people for a whopping $1.2 million. Yes, more than a million dollars. That's only $50 per person on average. Her cowbell is asking with vulnerability, and she accomplished something amazing with crowdsourcing and crowdfunding, but she learned the basics from street performance.

The arts is a tough path. You might be a great musician, but the percentage of these that become wealthy is relatively small. The same is even truer for painters.

Let's go back to Paul F. Thompkins, the comedian who agrees to perform if the number of tickets sold hits 150 or more. It's not unrealistic to guess he can gross $1,000 to $2,250 per show. A comedian like this could gross six figures a year without really even being famous.

What if you couch-surfed your way through your first few years of development as an artist, and grew your network in part because you stayed at people's houses? That's an interesting strategy. Check out couchsurfing.org and give it a shot!

## How a 30-Something Found His Passion and Turned It into a Six-Figure Job Surfing the Internet

"When I stand before God at the end of my life, I would hope that I would not have a single bit of talent left, and could say, 'I used everything you gave me.'" — Erma Bombeck

Brian's bachelor's degree in philosophy didn't make him very hirable in 1995. (Unfortunately, all the philosophy companies had gone out of business.) And the Internet, which was a big part of his destiny and his cowbell, was only the seed of what it would become. So he decided to go back to school for Oriental medicine and acupuncture.

He moved to San Diego and eventually completed a four-year master's degree in traditional Oriental medicine. Within a year of starting, he was amazed by the medicine and how little most Americans knew about it, so he started a website called The Pulse of Oriental Medicine to explain it in everyday terms. That website grew over time, and Brian learned a bit about SEO (search engine optimization —achieving free rankings in Google and other search engines).

By 2004, despite writing a book about Oriental medicine, having an acupuncture and herbal practice, and teaching medical terminology at the school he graduated from, he discovered he didn't like most of the realities of the practice of the medicine. He was too interested in science and testing. He didn't have the nurse-like caretaker personality that many acupuncture patients wanted.

At the same time, Brian had begun to allow Google to place advertisements on his site through the Google AdSense program. He received a check for $1,300 one month and began to pay more attention to growing website traffic. In December of 2004, he earned more than $5,000 from these ads.

So, he began to focus entirely on the website, letting his acupuncture practice dwindle. He analyzed his website analytics: What keywords could he get traffic for? Which ones would make him the most money? He discovered he didn't have to limit the site to Oriental medicine topics. And there were thousands of keywords his calculations told him he could make more money from.

He couldn't do all the writing himself, so he found more writers online and offered them 50% of the earnings on the articles they wrote. One writer sent him 100 articles in his first month. Two months in a row, Brian received checks for over $20,000. The following month, the situation changed with a Google algorithm change, one of the hardest SEO lessons Brian ever learned.

This was the beginning of Brian's Internet-related career, founded on his passions for both writing and Excel spreadsheet data and trend analysis (yeah, nerdy). The next five years were spent doing freelance Google ad management, serving as the e-commerce manager for outdoor retailer Adventure 16 in San Diego, then building and directing the search and social media department for a regional agency in Myrtle Beach, S.C. Since 2009 he has earned over six figures annually for that work. And that's how he found a lucrative career.

## Durable Competitive Advantage: Making Sure Your Company Isn't Unique Just Like All the Others

Widely considered the most successful investor in the 20th century, Warren Buffett is one of the richest and most influential people in the world. One reason for his success is that he didn't invest in a company unless it had what he called a "durable competitive advantage."

A competitive advantage empowers a company or person to outperform those who would steal its opportunities. A durable competitive advantage is a competitive advantage you're likely to be able to keep for many years. An advantage with true durability is one that is hard to steal!

The best durable competitive advantages have characteristics like these:

1.　　Exists in an industry with very little competition.
2.　　Sells a unique product or service that doesn't change much.
3.　　Provides a unique service that's difficult to replicate.
4.　　Is the low-cost buyer and seller of products the public constantly needs.
5.　　Spends little to no money on research and development.

You might not have all five. The more you have, the better.

Companies with some of these characteristics are Coca-Cola, H&R Block, and Walmart.

Coca-Cola's taste is unique. It hasn't changed much (except for that time they introduced New Coke, found out how important their original taste was, and went back). H&R Block does tax preparation, which hasn't changed much for a long time. The feature that H&R Block has that its competitors don't is a ton of locations all over the country. Walmart is a low-cost buyer and seller of many products the public constantly needs.

Let's go back to our talk show host example and look specifically at daytime talk show hosts.

1.　　Is there very little competition? Not really. You can easily google a chart of 26 of them.
2.　　Do they sell a unique product or service that doesn't change much? Yes, their personalities.
3.　　Do they provide a unique service that's difficult to replicate? No, not apart from the personalities.
4.　　Are they low-cost buyers and sellers of products the public constantly needs? No.
5.　　Do they spend little to no money on research and development? No.

So TV talk show hosts don't have a durable competitive advantage. In reality, very few companies or people do. Plus, technology can disrupt industries and dramatically weaken old structures, forcing them to adapt and grow. The Internet has done that to newspapers and the Yellow Pages. And more and more companies are finding they have to create content to compete, which has led certain industries to fight with other industries outside their normal borders.

Some pundits in recent years have asserted that competitive advantage is no longer possible. We, and many others, disagree. It's basically impossible for competition to exist without the possibility of advantage. If you have a number of identical giant, fat guys in line at a buffet, there is always one who is not only hungrier than the others but who has not eaten since he was kicked out of Golden Corral two days earlier. He will singlehandedly improve pork belly futures by reducing availability. The pundits are clearly confused, so let's be more specific.

You might not be able to find or create a 100% bulletproof dominance, but you can increase your competitive advantage by focusing on the right areas. The goal is to make it more likely people will choose you and less likely they'll depart for one of your competitors.

Here are some things you can focus on to improve your competitive advantage:

• Deepen and strengthen your relationship with customers
• Strive to understand customer problems more deeply and solve their problems quicker and more affordably
• Explore new win-win partnerships (often outside your industry or job function) that enable you to offer things other competitors can't
• Grow your personal network to increase your insight and resources
• Don't be obnoxious

Coincidentally, all of the above are Cowbell Principle fundamentals. This book will teach you how to do them better, increasing your competitive advantage.

## RAJIV SATYAL – FROM BUSINESS TO COMEDY

Rajiv Satyal is a former engineer and P&G marketer who has toured with Dave Chappelle, Tim Allen, Kevin Nealon, and Russell Peters. Rajiv has spoken to audiences from Fortune 50 companies (the top 50 companies in the Fortune 500) to NFL players on innovation, diversity, and personal branding. He runs a consulting business called the Standpoint Agency, which helps marketers generate insights for their brands.

When did Rajiv know he was funny? In 1985, in the third grade. His friend Ryan, who was the official class clown, always said Rajiv wasn't funny. Rajiv kept challenging Ryan, trying to get him to laugh. One day in the library, Ryan was singing "Di Di Dinosaur" and Rajiv sang back, "I don't wanna die!" Ryan fell on the floor laughing and then said, "Congratulations, now you're funny." Peer validation is really important! Rajiv previously thought he was funny; now he knew he was.

When did Rajiv know he wanted to be a comedian? Not until August 1998. At his brother's urging, he had entered the "Funniest Person in Cincinnati" Contest. He did really well, making the semifinals, and then he won the contest the next year.

When did Rajiv become a comedian? All of Rajiv's friends had a vision of him becoming a comedian before he did. At age 30 he moved to Los Angeles to work at Fiji water but hated it so much he left after 12 weeks. They gave him a check and asked what he was going to do. He could have gone back to Cincinnati and P&G but he said, "I don't think I ended up in L.A. for no reason. I'm going to stay here and be a stand-up comedian." He did a lot of introspection and meditation and walking around for a month, and then in October 2006 he started in earnest. Rajiv suggests that readers of this book take a few days to think about their purpose, their lives, and their passion; even if you just take one day off, go out somewhere and sit with it. This is such a big deal it's worth giving it at least one day!

When did Rajiv feel like he'd "made it"? His goal was to make enough money to support himself doing comedy, and he was able to get there in just two years, which is exceptionally fast. But he's still striving. His ideal job would be to work as a talk show host, preferably on TV… maybe on the web with a decent following. He has some big, hairy, audacious goals — to host the Oscars, for one. And he wants to leave the world with something, something people will quote him on. Oh yeah, Rajiv said that.

Rajiv's cowbell depends on the context. In life, it's comedy. For a club booker, he's a great host. "I think about everything and everyone at the club, not just the audience, though they are the most important," he notes. "But owner and wait staff are mandatory too." In show business, he thinks his cowbell might involve becoming a comedic host.

## GINI DIETRICH – SPINNING THE SPIN DOCTORS

Gini Dietrich is the founder and CEO of Arment Dietrich, a Chicago-based integrated marketing communications firm. She is the lead blogger at the PR and marketing blog, Spin Sucks, is co-author of Marketing In the Round, and is co-host of Inside PR, a weekly podcast about communications and social media. Her second book, Spin Sucks, is now available! (Que).

Gini confesses she started her business in 2005 without a vision or a real mission. She knew she wanted to build a global PR firm, but she had nothing that set her group apart. While they managed to grow a little bit (to $2 million in revenues), it was completely by accident. And then the economy tanked. Organizations could not only not afford to outsource communications, but they were also less willing to take a risk on a boutique agency. If they were going to outsource, they wanted the stability of a large and established firm. Gini knew her group had to do something … and fast.

Enter Spin Sucks. She says she started the blog simply to figure out the whole blogging thing and to see if it was something she could sell to potential clients. What happened was completely unexpected.

She and her colleagues had a vision: to change the perception that people have about the PR industry. PR professionals are too often referred to as spin doctors or liars because of a few bad apples when, in fact, a good majority of them are extremely ethical and educate clients away from unethical business practices. But, just like in any other industry, people love the train wrecks so the bad professionals always gain the limelight. Complicating the matter, in her opinion, is the fact that the industry just doesn't do a good job of, well, doing its own PR.

Unexpectedly, other PR professionals became her group's audience. And it's a polarized audience, she points out — people either get really angry or love her firm's message. (Gini once had a peer tell her that the unethical practices are just the way it's done and she should stop being so naive). Gini and company have made some enemies, but they also have one of the most engaged communities on the blogosphere. It also drives about 80% of Arment Deitrich's revenue (that's the business Gini started in 2005). Colleagues have called Gini and her group industry leaders, which drives a significant amount of brand awareness and new revenue. Today, the group is much more strategic and creates content for Spin Sucks, based on different audiences. It continues to fuel the group's growth, and Gini expects it will do so for the next several years.

## How To Put Chapter Two Into Action & Get The Results You Want

- Think about people you know who have a unique powerful skill. What is their cowbell?

- List all the stuff you love to do, at work or at home.

- Have you ever tried to sell something nobody wanted? What was it? What did they want instead? Was that a bagpipe?

- Do you think you might have any other bagpipes?

- What have you been paid for in the past? Why did people value those things?

## Hey You, Did You Get Your Free Cowbell Principle Bonuses?
As the owner of this book (even if you somehow got it for free) you are entitled to some awesome bonuses!

#1. The controversial chapter they made us take out! "You Can't Handle This Chapter: True Secrets of Success That Make People Uncomfortable" You may not want to read this one... it's very unconventional. But it's all so true that it's funny. And if you're the kind of person that just wishes people would level with you, you'll love it!

#2. The Superfun Cowbell Overview Webinar

#3. Mystery bonus! Better than mystery meat, guaranteed!

To get them, go to http://thecowbellprinciple.com/bonuses and opt in!

# 3. How To Find Out What People Really Want (Not What You Think They Want)

This is where mentorship meetings marketing. Mentors like Bruce Dickinson can guide us in using our cowbell to find and meet real demand. A number of free online tools can help us discover what people are really looking for. These two sources — mentors and marketing tools — are the subject of this chapter.

### Never Question The Bruce Dickinson

The Bruce Dickinson knows what people want. Bruce Dickinson is just like us — he puts on his pants one leg at a time — except after he puts on his pants he makes gold records.

What or who is your Bruce Dickinson? It's that thing or person who tells you what people want — your true north, your bellwether. Never question the Bruce Dickinson.

Bruce Dickinson is your most fanatic, most demanding, top 1% hungriest of fans. He's those girls who always screamed when they saw the Beatles. He's that dude in the crowd who tells Happy Gilmore, "You can do eet!" He is the cheering dad at the Little League game whose son is easily identified because his baseball glove is covering his face. When you find some fans, let them know you appreciate them. Exchange energy with them. No, that's not a euphemism.

Bruce Dickinson is credible. His opinion matters, and he's trying to make your life amazing. If this book helps you, I will be your Bruce Dickinson, at least a little bit. But you also need a real local, flesh-and-bones coach, mentor, or maybe even therapist, if you're really special. Find some sources of objectivity in your life (but who like you and see your talent) and give them the power to be the director/producer.

Sometimes we're too close to what we have to see what's good and what's not. Sometimes we're too hard on ourselves. Sometimes the people around us don't appreciate us.

Once his pants are on, Bruce Dickinson makes gold records. Be sure your source of insight and truth has produced results in the past. How many great albums happened when such-and-such producer came into the picture? That's why we need mentors and editors and coaches.

There's a difference between what you want to hear and what you need to hear. If you're down on yourself, like Gene Frenkle was, you need to hear the good stuff. If you're floating around in the helium of narcissism, like Buck Dharma was, you need to be brought back to earth. Bruce Dickinson can raise you up and he can burst your bubble.

Kevin Durant was recently named the NBA's MVP and gave what has been called one of the best sports speeches of all time. Without doubt, it is one of the best NBA MVP speeches of all time. He said to his mom, "We weren't supposed to be here. You're the real MVP."

Durant had a number of Bruce Dickinsons believing in his cowbell. His mother was the first. Durant also said to him teammate Nick Collison, "You knew I had potential. Every single day, I knew I could look at you and know that you respect me as a man, as a player, and that you would ride with me till the end. Thank you."

So find yourself some mentors. Sometimes you have to pay them, in which case we call them coaches.

But beware — there are some big-time hype-mongers who charge tons of money for their coaching and seminars. Brian views some of them with a lot of skepticism. And it's not totally from outside. He's bought some of those $2,000 online courses. He's been to live events where they pitch $10,000-per-month services. He's concluded that no matter how much value coaches can provide, there's only so much they can charge if they want to be ethical.

There are some coaches and speakers who take advantage of people; and even though those people are agreeing to do it, it's not right.

Seriously, some of the things we've said to clients or discovered for them about their customers are, without doubt, worth tens of thousands of dollars to them. But some customers of these infoproducts seem to be addicted to motivation and inspiration. They'll use credit cards and go bankrupt on hope, aided and abetted by speakers who do a good job of "selling from the stage."

Mind you, in some situations a $4,000 or $10,000 course or event makes sense. But there are few people who can and should pay that much for them.

You want to know how to evaluate a coach? Ask for references, same as you would any other employee. You want to see people who've succeeded with their help; you want to know the exact results that person got; and you want to hear it from that person, not from the coach.

If the only person their "system" has helped is the coach, how do we know it will work for you?

"It worked for me so it will work for anybody" is questionable logic. Maybe the coach had an advantage or talent you don't. Brian has occasionally joked about writing a self-help book called "How to Succeed Like Me If You Start With All the Talents And Advantages I Had."

From the start, you want to know that the approach the coach is selling has worked for many people or companies. When Brian and his team taught his FanReach Facebook Marketing Series in 2011, they had students get profits from their courses on Facebook posting and advertising. Only after they saw that did they create a course about profiting from Facebook. Even though they had made money from marketing the course on Facebook, that wasn't proof enough for them.

The point is that you want to find a mentor or coach who's really out for your best interests. If you have to buy into a system, make sure it has benefitted a lot of people already. If you want to be a guinea pig, that's fine, but go into that with your eyes open.

### Mentors Are Crucial: Who Is Your Bruce Dickinson?

If you've never had a mentor, you probably aren't that successful. I'm sure there are exceptions. But consider — have you never had a parent mentor you? A teacher? A coach?

If you haven't, this is a serious issue. People need each other. Human beings are a social species. We need each other's help.

Some people have a tough time asking for or receiving help. They always want to be the helper and consequently might not have a mentor. But here's a question that points out the hypocrisy of that attitude: If helping people feels good to you, who are you to deny others the opportunity to help you and thus to feel as good as you do when you help people?

Even Batman, one of the most individualistic of our fictional heroes, had mentors. Andy Livengood, one of Brian's comedy writing partners, explains that in the comics they call it the "bat family." See, there really are people nerdier than Brian! Every fictional military hero had military training — drill instructors, and others.

According to Joseph Campbell, the fourth stage of "The Hero's Journey" is to find a mentor. The mentor gives the potential hero confidence, advice, or training. Luke had Obi-Wan. Superman had his father's fortress of solitude. Spiderman had Uncle Ben. Batman had Liam Neeson.

But we still have myths of men who had no training, were special from birth, and conquered any odds. Cowboys. Gunfighters born with lightning speed. We've encountered these unmentored special-from-birth victors in fiction but not in reality. But rarely in reality is talent alone enough to achieve greatness. The good news is that even the moderately talented can achieve great things if they have good mentorship and practice and work hard enough, long enough.

This book is part of your training and should boost your confidence.

What about the flip side? Can we become overdependent upon mentors? Certainly. See earlier discussion of gurus who unethically fleece people of money. It's wise to understand that there are stages of dependence, times when you need advice and you need encouragement. That's awesome. But it's healthy to move beyond it at some point. Stand on your own. Apply the advice.

If you need a mentor, ask. Sometimes people do it for free. Sometimes it's a trade. Sometimes it's paid.

Brian has had tons of mentors, to one degree or another:

• His dad taught him to work consistently ("Mow the lawn every week if you want an allowance"). He taught Brian to do a good job (he taught Brian to wash dishes thoroughly, explaining how his own father had taught him the same way; Brian felt like he was in the military for a second — "That dish isn't clean, Private!"). When Brian moved to San Diego with a girl who couldn't keep a job and needed to borrow money, his dad sent it, but with a note ("As you go through life, consider how your actions affect the people around you") that stuck with him and taught him a lesson.

• Brian's mom taught him to know and express his feelings, to examine them, and to have an interior spiritual life.

• Brian's coauthor, Garrison Wynn, taught him how to balance humor and professionalism (not all of Brian's crazy videos need to be public, and some of his edgier jokes shouldn't be in a keynote) and has given him innumerable other tips on becoming an outstanding speaker.

• Garrison's coauthor, Brian Carter, helped him navigate and update his social media approach and let him know that it was not his fault that computers seem to want to destroy his life.

When you find a source of truth and insight, trust it. Never question what people say they like or don't like, because this information — what they want and what they will pay for — is your compass.

Sometimes people question your gift and you doubt it. You need a Bruce Dickinson to stand up for the value of it. Now, some people would argue that you don't need the approval of others to be successful. Unfortunately, those people are rarely listened to because almost no one approves of their opinion.

Even companies sometimes need outside views to give them perspective. That's why they hire consultants and why executives hire coaches.

## Stuff Humans Like

There are some things all people want, regardless of culture. We all need air, water, and food. Check out Maslow's pyramid — we need shelter, sex, love, and self-realization.

Once we take care of the basics, we want to:

• Have friends
• Laugh
• Love someone and be loved
• Make a difference
• Leave a legacy
• Have our efforts appreciated

Sometimes we can feel guilty for having goals like "write a fiction bestseller" because there are people whose goal is to "get clean water today" or "find food for my child." It bugs us that the people with money and power haven't already done more to help Africa. We've done small things like contribute to Tweetsgiving through Epic Change, or buy goats or wells for villages on behalf of a family member as their Christmas gift. But is that enough?

The truth is that guilt as a motivator has limitations and is often misplaced.

One of Brian's cousins used to do missions to Cuba, and he supported her as he was able. His heart is with them. Garrison has been in the streets of Third World cities and in the rainforests of rural Africa and Indonesia. He understands what poverty and zero opportunity actually look (and smell) like.

In America we have amazing opportunities in every way. Even if we're held back by crime or mental and emotional disorders, there are free programs that can help. Some people slip through the cracks but have nowhere near the kind of obstacles that Somalis do. Organized crime and bulimia only exist in countries that have a lot to steal and enough to eat.

## Taste Is Subjective

There are a lot of weird things that only a few people like and a lot of normal things that a lot of people hate.

Things that some people love and other people hate:

- Southerners
- The band Rush
- Vegetarianism
- Pork products
- PETA
- Fish tanks
- Sarah McLachlan
- Kathie Lee Gifford
- Nicolas Cage
- River Dancing
- Accents
- Figs
- Religion
- Boxer briefs
- Eggplant
- Sarcasm
- Lists

Not everybody will have a fever for your cowbell. Your cowbell is only for people who love your cowbell. If you want to make money with it, it's got to be something a lot of people like. Or a few people with a lot of money. Or one dude who can make everyone like it.

But the good news is that there are very few things that everyone likes. Many of us shake our heads at the things that the mainstream likes, like Katy Perry, reality shows, and malls.

You have to be able to put yourself in the shoes of people who might like your cowbell.

Having no perspective about your own culture is just as bad as not being able to put yourself in your customers' shoes. Some people are, in fact, unable to do it. The only way they ever put themselves in the shoes of others is when they go bowling. Understanding how others feel might not come naturally to everyone, but it's a requirement if you want to influence anyone.

## Stuff Americans Like

Let's get outside our normal lens for a minute, just for perspective. Perspective will help you put yourself in your customers' shoes.

NASCAR, cheerleaders, peanut butter and jelly, lawsuits, big cars, Seinfeld, ice, guns, being thin or fat, American football, over-sweetening, working too much, paying ridiculous sums for college, censoring sex but not violence, fast food, expensive slow food, treating pets like humans, treating children like pets, having a World Series with mostly American teams, and calling small-city airports that require two connections to get to "international." (We're looking at you, Charleston!)

## What the Rest of the World Thinks Is Stupid about Americans

True or not, here are a few stereotypes about Americans. This list is mainly for Americans to use to get that aforementioned perspective that can lead to making more money by empathizing with others.

Americans are fat. They like everything big, including their stomachs. They play sports that no other countries play. They're rude and loud and obnoxious. The money's all the same color. The speed limits change everywhere. They're oversensitive to honest feedback. They love the word awesome, fake smiles, tipping, Waffle House, advertising, stereotypes (unless it's a stereotype of them), big corporations, being in a hurry, punctuality, money, gigantic restaurant portions, loud TV preachers, and a brand of English that is like so totally littered with like overly repeated crutch words that it's like totally awesome! Like, you know?

## Stuff Other Countries Like about Americans

Okay, let's balance it out with what the rest of the world likes about us.

We're known (and liked) for being friendly, experimenting and innovating, dreaming, wanting others to succeed and do well, creating awesome music, actually having customer service, caring if strangers around you get hurt, creating and contributing to the Internet, speaking clearly, and showering daily. Other countries also like our ability to change, our work ethic, equality, ambition, microbrews, personal freedom, self-help, pragmatism, big houses, coffee everywhere, cheese, optimism, tendency to buy anything when we're on vacation, passion, open-mindedness, conferences, and friends.

Okay, now that we've separated ourselves a bit from culture, let's look at what your potential customers like.

**If You Liked Graph Paper in School, You'll Love Graph Search!**

Graph Search might sound intimidating to some people (the ones who cheated on math tests), so let's explain what it really is.

Facebook lets you search for some really cool things. It has all this data about how all people on Facebook are connected to their friends and what they like and what their friends like. They call it the Open Graph, because it's a graph of our connections that's open for people to look at, either with Graph Search or by programming apps.

In a way, we all are in different tribes based on what we like. There are the Apple people and the PC people, for example. But we all have overlapping likes. In fact, a lot of people use both Apple and PC or Microsoft products.

Often the people we are friends with only share two or three major likes with us. A lot of people like very particular things (like the band Rush) that they never really share in community with others, unless they go to a big concert or conference.

Graph Search is a cool way to learn about your audience or your target market — the people you want paying for your cowbell.

Try this out: Think of one of your favorite Facebook pages… and if you can't think of one, let's try CNN or Fox News. Go to the Facebook search box, type in "Pages liked by people who like" and then add the Facebook page. The search will return a whole bunch of other things that the fans of that thing like.

For example, let's compare what the Fox News fans like with what the CNN fans like.

What's more unique? Fox News fans like Mitt Romney, Sarah Palin, Paul Ryan, CNN, George Strait, Jesus Christ, Brad Paisley, the Bible, Macy's, The Hangover, Disney, Zac Brown Band, Jesus Loves You, Jeff Dunham, Blake Shelton, Mark Wahlberg… Among these results, country music is a pretty unique thing, and the Republican candidates are no surprise.

CNN fans like App Center, Bill Gates, Facebook Security, Michael Phelps, Twitter, The Ellen DeGeneres Show, Google, Facebook Studio, Steve Jobs, snowboarding, Funny or Die, Breaking Bad, The Official Grumpy Cat… We find much more technology and comedy high in the list.

What do they have in common? Fans of both pages like the New York Times, BBC News, Barack Obama, Upworthy, George Takei, CNN, Fox News, Amazon.com, Target, Facebook, YouTube, NFL, ESPN, History

Network, photography, Will Ferrell, National Geographic, camping, Subway, music, Moody Blues, Cars (the movie), Johnny Cash… These are things we can consider to be pretty popular with a lot of Americans on Facebook.

Interesting, isn't it?

What if we looked at what Apple fans like versus what Microsoft fans like?

Or cat people versus dog people?

There's a lot to be learned about your potential audience.

Here are a few guidelines to get the best results:

• Graph Search results aren't returned in any special order. We can assume it's by popularity.

• You'll get more objective search results if you create a new Facebook account with no friends or likes. Otherwise, you're more likely to see things that you and your friends like.

• It's always best to compare two or three things at once (like we did with CNN vs. Fox). You'll find the things they all like. Remove those. The ones that are more unique will teach you more about your audience.

You can search for other things with Graph Search. Here are some example searches:

• Interests liked by fans of George Takei
• Pages liked by people who work at Walmart
• Interests liked by people who work at Sony
• Pages liked by people who majored in accounting
• Pages liked by people who majored in accounting and live in the United States
• Pages liked by people who are my age
• Pages liked by people who are over 40 years old
• Pages liked by people who are married
• Pages liked by people who are single and under 30 years old
• Pages liked by people who have been to Lincoln Memorial
• Pages liked by people who were born in Dayton, Ohio
• Pages liked by people who live in Charleston, S.C.

Don't forget to narrow your search. In any search results, look to the right and you'll see you can narrow the results with a variety of factors.

## You're a Tool If You Don't Use the AdWords Keyword Tool (How to

## Find Out What People Are Really Looking For)

The AdWords Keyword Planner is a tool that tells you what people are searching Google for, and how many of them are searching each phrase per month. This kind of tool came along with search engines not too long after the new millennium and created a revolution in market research. Suddenly, we knew how many people were googling to "buy a bike online" and how many wanted to "buy a Trek" compared to "buy a Schwinn." It's that kind of data that helped Brian earned more than $20,000 a month from Google AdSense in 2005. And that data has propelled many businesses from obscurity to the kind of success that demands attention and respect.

You can use this tool yourself to see what exactly people are looking for in your niche. Once you understand what they want and how much they want it compared to other things, you can make smarter business decisions. For example, if you're starting a local retail store, you can check how many people search monthly for each type of product in your region, which might help you decide how much of each product to buy to stock your store.

To get started with the AdWords Keyword Planner, go to https://adwords.google.com/KeywordPlanner. The fastest way to get started, if you have a website, is to put that in and see what it comes up with. If you get stuck, Google has a great help screen for getting started at https://support.google.com/adwords/answer/2999770?hl=en.

Before you skip it, we feel compelled to tell you that 100% of people who've never used a tool like this are wrong about what people are looking for, how they're searching for it, what words they use to describe it, and what they want most. It's a big paradigm shift, and you need to see the data to understand it. Use this tool, or a competitor of yours will, and they'll use its insights to beat you in the business arena.

## Google Trends

Want to know what's popular and what's growing fastest? Check out Google Trends. It'll tell you what gets searched the most and whether it's growing fast or not. In which countries and cities is that thing most popular? What related terms are trending? You can type in your own ideas and see if they're popular and if they're growing or shrinking. Or you can browse through the fastest-growing topics in categories like business & politics, entertainment, lifestyle, nature & science, shopping & fashion, sports, or travel & leisure.

For example, according to our search on May 20, 2014,

• Barack Obama is the most searched politician, but Manny Pacquiao is the political figure with the fastest-growing search.

• Donald Sterling is unfortunately the most searched person in entertainment.

• Frozen is the most searched movie but Captain America: Winter Soldier has had the most growth.

• Pizza is the most searched food. Delivery, anyone? Man, I'm hungry. Wouldn't this book go a lot better with some pizza? Mmmm. Pepperoni, sauce, crust, mmmm. So good. (You're welcome pizza franchises. No need to reimburse us for this.)

• New York City is the most searched city, but Boston is the fastest-growing search.

• Dogs are the most searched animal (they are, after all, man's best friend) but rabbits are the fastest-growing animal search (can we say they're multiplying?).

• On kids' TV, SpongeBob SquarePants is the biggest search but Young Justice is trending highest.

• Skrillex is the most searched DJ but Frankie Knuckles is trending. And that is the best name ever. Sounds more like a mafia enforcer, doesn't it?

That's interesting but not necessarily helpful. You should start with the things you're interested in. Type them into the Google Trends search bar. You can compare multiple searches. For example, you can check out "Which thing are people most interested in: self-help, success, or making money?" Turns out it's success. If you're focused on self-help, you can compare whether self-help or personal growth is the more popular term. (It's self-help.)

Type in some of your interests, talents, and skills and see what you find.

Are there outdated cowbells? Yes, cowbells are obsolete when people no longer have a fever for them. Examples: handshake buzzers, the Walkman, women over 50… just kidding! But seriously, the 40th or 50th birthday used to be a death knell for actresses, but now a number of TV series use older women more prominently. Being a great older actress can be a cowbell in itself.

When you're looking at trends, don't just look for the most popular. Really explore that niche with multiple searches and see which one has been growing at the highest rate for a year or two. That way, your investments of time and money in that area are more likely to pay off.

Knowing what people are interested in is the key to being able to establish your own value. If you don't know what people really think about, there is a pretty good chance you won't be on their mind.

## PAMELA GALLE — TRY WHAT YOU'RE AFRAID OF

The reputation of Charleston, S.C.'s Threshold Repertory Theatre is professional and colorful — in large part due to the vision of the artistic director Pamela Galle. Galle, whose resume includes actress, producer, and director, has been involved in the theater industry for 20 years, during which she has worn a wide variety of hats, both physical and metaphorical. In Pam's words…

I knew I wanted to do something with passion, but I didn't know what it was. In fifth and sixth grades, I wrote plays and forced my friends to be in them.

As an adult, I worked in the corporate world for a while and wasn't very good at it, although I didn't realize that until later. I tried teaching preschool because I had that mothering instinct. I tried making furniture. I renovated the interior of a house with crown molding and tiles and cabinets, but that wasn't it.

Later, I was attending a small church when the choir director expressed a need for singers and asked if I'd help. I said okay but I was very afraid of it, so I'd pretend to be a character and that kind of worked. I thought, "Hmm… maybe I'll take an acting class." I went to Oglethorpe University and took some classes. I did one monologue. Then I got pregnant and my husband got sick with melanoma. We moved to Charlotte. Gilbert got over melanoma.

I took a summer acting class and the teacher said, "I think if you auditioned, you'd get work." I did a community theatre show and fell in love with it. I got bit, as in, infatuated! I found an agent in Charlotte. The first show I did was a community theater show, directed by the founder of the only equity theater in Charlotte. I got into the second play I auditioned for. It was a professional show, and I had no background. I was way over my head, but I made it through. It's different when you're young in the public eye versus older; when you're older, there's no excuse for not knowing what you're doing, so I got blasted in the reviews. That was overwhelming. I'd never experienced that kind of public humbling. But I started doing more community theater. I was confused and frustrated and I stopped getting work. I couldn't get hired.

That went on for a year and a half, and then I woke up one day at 3 a.m. and said, "Well, then I'll produce a play." I had no money. I started saving money. I also had no play. My agent, Judy Cook, was a writer so I asked her if she had any plays or ideas. She had an idea — and in two and a half weeks she wrote the play Cerulean Blues. We staged it in a black box theater and it was successful.

My whole approach changed because now I was a producer. I realized I had been a pain in the ass as an actor, so that changed and then I got more parts. That equity theater died for political reasons. So I thought, "I'll start a theater company." Two friends who were playwrights joined me in that for three years. Then my marriage fell apart, and we separated.

I think my cowbell, though, is in acting. I've done it more, done it longer. I have the credentials; I've won awards and been nominated numerous times. I've never been paid to produce. Producing shows well is a forte of mine, but maybe not so much the marketing or running of a company with a physical space. I have the Threshold Repertory Theater in Charleston. I've done more directing here, and I'm grateful for that because it's easier to be an actor without credentials than a director. I had directed a few times in Charlotte but more in Charleston. There are so many companies in Charleston, you can get stuck in your own. Sometimes I act at Pure Theater.

Soon I'm moving to Los Angeles to just act, although I will continue to support Threshold for a year. I think my cowbell was always in theater, when I consider that I was writing the plays in fifth and sixth grades. The people I talk to will often say they were around 10 years old when they began to latch onto something they loved. People who haven't found it, I ask, "What were you in love with at the age of 10?" Often it's something artistic.

## DAVID BURROWS – A DYSLEXIC COPYWRITER?

David's Twitter bio says: Creative, social, snarky kind of guy. Former Yahoo!. VP of Marketing PR at Cinsay. Filmmaker, wine collector. He says…

I was born and raised in Dallas and I have a Wikipedia page. People seek me out for humor, branding and marketing copy writing- but that wasn't always true.

I wrote some copy to sell my Mercedes on Craigslist. A friend of mine at a magazine shared it and then an auto blog picked it up, then Yahoo Autos picked it up, then Business Insider picked it up!

Here are a few excerpts:

"I have personally driven this car from San Diego to Dallas on an almost non-stop road trip. The steering wheel is big, fluid and offers just enough resistance and connection to the road to give you the impression that you are not only in charge of the car, but also of your entire life's destiny. Driving it for any distance is empowering and can make you feel you can go anywhere. In fact, this car has plowed effortlessly through Death Valley, dodged falling rocks in Arizona, stared into the depths of the Grand Canyon and climbed mountainous icy hills in Colorado.

"One of the most outstanding features of this car is that it starts -- anytime, anywhere. Whether it's 105* or -5*, F the car's engine turns over and roars to life with one simple twist of the key. There's no fumbling, cranking, pumping the pedal, stalling or waiting for the zombies to come and kill you. Fact: This car would NEVER be featured as a get-away-car in a zombie horror film because it would get you away from whatever is trying to eat, dissolve, melt, vaporize, mate, shoot or kill you."

I was contacted by a bunch of people, including a teacher in Austin teacher who wanted me to come talk about creative writing. People were emailing and calling and I'm like, "I'm just trying to sell my Mercedes!"

When I wrote it I was channeling Robert Deniro and Jon Stewart– what would they say to each other, then amalgamate that into one voice.

Humor was the iron shield of Thor for me in grade school. I learned that if I made people laugh, they wouldn't hit me or lock me in the closet. I mostly write self-deprecating humor, which by the way, doesn't work for corporations.

I was a NASA ambassador in Dallas. That didn't really fit. I spoke at schools. It involved a lot of math and math is not a big fan of me, which you can see in our finances. I had to talk about difficult formulas to describe the things I loved about space. This kept me from going into science.

I tried acting too, in college. I got walk-on roles to help raise money with Sony for their non-profit. I realized with acting, you're going to be poor for a long time and put all your time into it. I'm more comfortable behind a camera or writing.

I worked with Tim Sanders at Pat Summerall Productions selling scholastic video shoots. Broadcast.com told me to come over AudioNet, Mark Cuban's company. I interviewed with Mark and got hired in a week.

Now I do creative writing for myself. I help my wife and friends with their businesses. I write copy for Cinsay or its partners.

Writing is about finding a new perspective. We have memories in our head: Films, people playing characters, and strong images of characters and scenes. So plug them into your story.

For press releases it's more objective obviously. I do a lot of writing- all the copy on cinsay.com and PowerPoints- every press release we've had.

This writing cowbell is only 20% of what I do- I've discovered it more recently. I'm dyslexic and ADD- so it's a challenge for my writing and proofreading. My English teachers are spinning in their wheelchairs or graves.

10 years ago I got better at it and wrote a personal blog about my life and who I saw and experiences I had. That became more interesting and

creative the more I practiced it. It leaked into things I was doing in my career.

Also, I got appointed to Baylor College as an Arts & Sciences board member to help take their film department to the next level. The Film department has been stuck in the Radio & TV department. They're now going to create a formal department of film with a chair and an endowment and part of a building dedicated to it.

**How To Put Chapter Three Into Action And Get The Results You Want**

- Using your list of things you love to do, go to AdWords Keyword Tool (Google it!) and enter your list, see what keywords come back.

- Which are most popular? Do they surprise you? What does this mean for what you should build or develop in yourself or your business?

- Which things are people not looking for? These might be bagpipes.

- Which keywords have the highest suggested bid? These are the keywords people compete over because there's value and revenue there.

- Go to Google Trends and see which keywords are growing, maintaining or declining.

- Go do Graph Search and see what your potential buyers like.

- Go to the Facebook Audience Insights tool in Ad Manager and put in people or businesses that you would like to emulate- find out about their fans.

**Hey You, Did You Get Your Free Cowbell Principle Bonuses?**
As the owner of this book (even if you somehow got it for free) you are entitled to some awesome bonuses!

#1. The controversial chapter they made us take out! "You Can't Handle This Chapter: True Secrets of Success That Make People Uncomfortable" You may not want to read this one... it's very unconventional. But it's all so true that it's funny. And if you're the kind of person that just wishes people would level with you, you'll love it!

#2. The Superfun Cowbell Overview Webinar

#3. Mystery bonus! Better than mystery meat, guaranteed!

To get them, go to http://thecowbellprinciple.com/bonuses and opt in!

# 4. Opposition: If You Haven't Made A Few Enemies, You're Probably Not That Good

It's natural to pause when we're opposed, and then question ourselves. But because of opposition, we are refined and we gain confidence. When you encounter a new source of opposition or a greater degree of opposition than you've seen before, your growth process repeats. When you have no opposition, you may be going with the flow, fitting in constructively — or you may be giving in too much and conforming to an unhealthy degree. Without competition, it is difficult to get better.

### The Enemies of the Cowbell

In the "More Cowbell" sketch, was there ever too much cowbell? The band initially thought so. Why?

You get the sense from the singer that Gene is stealing his spotlight. Similarly, close to you, there may be people who think you're wrong. Some of them will be jealous. Don't let them convince you to hide your light. Shine your light and demand a part.

The tables may reverse at times. Sometimes you're going to rain on someone else's parade — right or wrong.

It can be disappointing to see how some of the people you work or compete with react on your journey to success. When you are struggling, they want to help; when you are average, they want to encourage you to get better; when you are good, they applaud and support you; and when it's clear that you're super talented and you start getting recognition from your industry, they get weird and might not be so happy for you. It's like the Oscar-nominated actor who loses, clapping for Meryl Streep as she wins yet again. The hands are happy and the smile that made this runner-up famous is on bright mode. But her eyes clearly say "Crap!"

## Dealing with Cowbell Haters

If you don't have enemies, you don't matter. We've seen many shy away from that next step toward greatness because they want so much to be liked. They don't want any enemies. But if you stand for anything, you absolutely will have enemies. They don't have to be an archnemesis. It doesn't have to be violent opposition. It might be passive-aggressive. Someone might gossip behind your back.

If you just want friends, become a Buddhist and stop pursuing material things. Become a communist and stop trying to have more stuff than others. Join a church and stop lusting after anything except spiritual greatness. But even Jesus said his followers should expect enemies; and Jesus himself was not Mr. Popular with the masses during his earth tour.

Power and fame always attract detractors. Roadblocks that stop the average sharpen the skills of the great.

"People just don't understand how obsessed I am with winning. Everything negative — pressure, challenges — is all an opportunity for me to rise." — Kobe Bryant

Sometimes in a championship series you'll see a member of one team talk down in the media about a star on another team. This can backfire, spurring the dissed star to an unstoppable performance in the next game. Competitive types often use detractors as fuel to work harder and prove themselves. If you want to be a star, use every failure and personal attack to increase your intensity, practice harder, and win.

## If You Don't Have Enemies, You Don't Matter

"You have enemies? Good. That means you've stood up for something, sometime in your life." — Winston Churchill

When Brian first began blogging and speaking at Internet marketing conferences, it wasn't long before he received some criticism, some of which seemed emotional and unreasonable. And some of it might have come from how he wrote and spoke. He had some crazy ideas for making his talks unique and illustrating his points.

At the Scary SEO conference in 2008, Brian pretended to hypnotize a coworker he'd brought with him, and had him slap himself. It was an absurd example of influence meant only to create a laugh.

At Pubcon Vegas in 2008, he gave away a pink stuffed pony as the prize in a small Twitter contest. Then the woman who won the pony had a bunch of pictures taken with microfamous Internet marketers. She sent them to Brian and he wrote a blog post about it. There was a lot of criticism that this wasn't a useful post. Perhaps they saw the tactics as too obvious. It didn't really matter; it yielded a lot of interaction and buzz. Sometimes when you succeed, other people are jealous, especially if they have internal rules that keep them from doing it the way you did. (See Amy Plumber's TED talk about people yelling at her to "get a job!")

Brian talked it over with his agency CEO at the time. His CEO said, "If you don't have haters, you probably aren't really putting yourself out there."

Brian also pinged Rand Fishkin about it. Rand is CEO of Moz, then called SEOMoz, and had ascended to his microfame not long before. Rand said, "I definitely agree with your CEO. When we had no haters, we were too small to be significant."

## Haters Gonna Hate

You can't make everyone happy. Even celebrated leaders have detractors.

Think about how many people have stood up for something and not long after were assassinated: Martin Luther King, Jr.; John F. Kennedy; Mahatma Gandhi; John Lennon. If these great people were killed for fighting major cultural and political trends, isn't it reasonable you might at least get a few negative Facebook comments for being honest or for striving for something big?

A useful psychological principle for understanding this phenomenon is projection. Wikipedia says it's "the act or technique of defending oneself against unpleasant impulses by denying their existence in oneself, while attributing them to others. For example, a person who is rude may constantly accuse other people of being rude." Another way to put it is that we blame other people for our own failings.

If you've ever been jealous of someone else's achievements, you've been on the hater side of it. What's a hater? Urban Dictionary says a hater is "a person who simply cannot be happy for another person's success. It's hard to avoid being a hater when you're unhappy with your own life."

Another example people give for this is the crabs-in-the-bucket analogy. Seafood chefs can place a certain number of crabs into a bucket without a lid, and they'll never get out. The reason is that as one crab tries to walk on the others to reach the top, a crab below it pulls it back down by trying to ascend itself. This teaches us two lessons: Don't walk on others to get to the top, and trying to pull down the people ahead of you isn't constructive for either person. You would think the human race had risen above this type of behavior, but the truth is we have to personally make the effort to conduct ourselves with civility in the crab bucket we call society. It's just like life in the big city: The smell and walking sideways may be unavoidable, but how we treat others is up to us. (That last sentence mercifully ends the crab metaphor.)

If you have strong dreams or ambitions and are stuck — not actively pursuing them — you will be vulnerable to jealous hater behavior. Your own unfulfilled potential can create that. Do you secretly have a list of people you think don't deserve the fruits of their labor? It's more constructive to congratulate successful people and build relationships with them. That's the win-win.

## Any Truth to the Criticism?

Regardless of why haters hate, their criticism can prove useful. Can you learn anything from their comments?

Whenever Brian — who has already admitted his tendency to analyze everything — encounters negativity, he files that input away for later examination, but he also asks himself: "Is this person just pushing his personal baggage onto me?"

Later, examining their perspective, you will find that they have good input (maybe you need to revise your approaches in some way) or they don't. The biggest pitfall here is that if their criticism works with any of your own fears or negative self-perceptions, their shit may reinforce your shit.

So you also have to work on your shit. Discover your fears about yourself and find the truths so that their shit can't stick to your shit.

For example, suppose you've often feared that maybe you're not really that special. Maybe you're not that smart. Or that funny. Maybe you feel like a fake. Those are some really powerful fears that can stop you from moving forward. So you have to go through each one.

1.    Fear that you're not special enough to have a cowbell.
2.    Fear that you're a fake.
3.    Fear of the big moment.

## Finding the True and the False in Your Fears

Let's look at some of those fears and see what we can learn from them.

### I'm Afraid I'm Not That Special

Am I not that special? That's a tough one. How can you prove you're special? Aren't we all special? Is it that I'm trying to achieve something in rarefied air that maybe only more special people deserve? How about I just do what I'm good at and what I love and accept whatever happens? Do yo thang and accept whatever the fruits are and aren't.

The flip side of this one is this: Don't think you're better than other people. This one is a huge struggle. It's politically correct to say we're all equal. But we're not. Brian can't dunk like an NBA player. But a ton of people can't write as much as he does. So we all have different areas of genius. We are not clones.

But are we all genius to equal degree? That may be impossible to answer. If a guy just delivers pizza and plays video games his whole life and seems happy with it, is he as genius as Einstein or Tony Robbins or even Barack Obama? No, I don't think so. Mr. Slacker is not a genius like Mr. Einstein. Whether he was born that way or should have tried harder, he has not accomplished as much. He has not helped the world as much as Einstein.

If we are all born to be uniquely powerful, joyful, and helpful, then maybe the biggest crime in life is not developing your own potential. Submitting to your fears and laziness is depriving the rest of the world. And you are poorer, too, for not growing and learning, accomplishing and helping.

Let's look at one more of those fears.

## I'm Afraid I'm a Fake

Am I a fake? Maybe you've heard of impostor syndrome. Wikipedia says it is "a psychological phenomenon in which people are unable to internalize their accomplishments. Despite external evidence of their competence, those with the syndrome remain convinced that they are frauds and do not deserve the success they have achieved. Proof of success is dismissed as luck, timing, or as a result of deceiving others into thinking they are more intelligent and competent than they believe themselves to be."

This is a big problem for people who want more out of life, who want to become and achieve more, because you're going to succeed and accomplish things. You're going to feel good about those things sometimes. You're going to doubt yourself other times. Could I achieve that again? Was it just luck and timing? It's easy to fear you're an impostor when you know you're always working on your bio.

Let's back up for a second.

Brian pretty much knew from the time he was 16 that he wanted to be somebody else or something more. He wanted to achieve something. He wanted to transform. His first thought in this direction was "I want to be a famous rock guitarist soloing on stage."

Right now at 40, having accomplished a number of notable things, he still wants more and different accomplishments. It's doubtful this will change. If it does, it does. Maybe he'll get tired. Or maybe he'll have some spiritual revelation that none of it matters. (Sometimes this "spiritual" idea is difficult to differentiate from depression.) Until then, he remains hungry for life.

So all that means is that for the last 24 years he has tried to be a 45-degree angle line on a chart of success.

He learned along the way that he needed a "platform" and a "bio" and "credibility markers." Look at any successful author or speaker or expert website. Look at any LinkedIn profile. We accumulate this proof that we're useful, powerful, and important. That we matter. That you should pay attention to us. That you should pay us. Whether you're just doing something for your bio/resume or you did it for another reason, these things all accumulate in your bio.

As you develop that bio, you are faced with questions: Is this who I am? Is that the real me? I don't always feel as awesome as my bio. Is it for real? Am I a fake?

Few people are spared this dance with doubt. Garrison, too, went through career-finding phases, from stock transfer agent to show business to sales to marketing to corporate leader to show biz again, until he put it all together and started a company that specializes in training, consulting, and delivering keynotes at events. Even after a good measure of success in this custom-designed niche he built, he acknowledges that it's easy to look back on your life and read your bio and wonder, "Who the heck is this guy? Is this for real? What this experience really qualifies me for is…?"

However, that's your brain telling you a lie. Someone else looks at that bio and says, "A former Fortune 500 leader with a good track record in multiple industries who was also touring professional comedian? Yeah, this dude should speak at our conference!"

If the real you is the you that you used to be, then yes, you are fake. You are who you were, plus your potential, plus what you've accomplished. Those accomplishments may be past, gone, dead. But they happened. They are indicative of who you are and what you're capable of. So, no, you are not a fake. The only truly fake person is a cardboard cutout. And even those usually represent a real person…or at least a well-meaning fictional person selling something that's apparently really hard to notice.

Ultimately, if you lie in your bio, yes, you are a fake. Yet, even a BS bio is proof you are ambitious. With that kind of drive, wouldn't the truth be an even better advantage?

Now, if your bio is honest, you just need to own your accomplishments.

Not being able to internalize your accomplishments means you believe who you used to be is more real than who you are now. But whatever your experience has been over the years, you are most likely more valuable right now.

Pat yourself on the back. Congratulate yourself. Give yourself a hug.

Maybe you didn't get enough of that from your parents. Who knows? Who cares! Re-parent yourself now.

Close your eyes and imagine one of your accomplishments. Shake your own hand. Look yourself in the eye and say "good job." Point both index fingers at that you and say "you da man."

Switch perspectives and see yourself being congratulated. Is your brain saying "yeah, but…"? Slap yourself in the face. Hear someone tell you, "You did this. Stop being a dumbass. Enjoy it. Good job. We want to celebrate this with you. Run a victory lap. Put your hands up like you just won a race, because you did."

If that doesn't help, welcome to the Impostor's Club. Just get on with it and move forward. Because, in truth, impostor syndrome doesn't have to stop you. Fake it till you make it; believe it till it comes true.

Many people who are phonier but less talented than you are have been extremely successful. Stop stopping yourself from moving forward. The big question you have to ask yourself is this: Others have overcome all this stuff; why would that not be you? Why should that be someone else and not you? Why not you?

## Fear of the Big Moment: Are You Clutch?

Ray Allen is probably the best three-point shooter in basketball history. He's hit the most of them. He's also one of the most clutch shooters in history.

What is clutch? Clutch is performing optimally when the pressure is on, when the performance is most needed. Game-winning shots. LeBron, Kobe, Nowitzki, and Durant are also on this list with Ray.

When the pressure is on, either you're clutch, or you choke.

So what makes clutch performers? What are they thinking about?

Ray Allen said this: "As much as people talk about all the shots I hit to win games, I don't remember those. I remember the ones that I didn't make. That's what keeps me in the gym."

Do you think you're an impostor? Do you obsess over your failures? Are you thinking about what you need to improve? Good, you have the clutch mindset.

There's a huge debate over whether clutch is innate or can be learned. Our experience is that you can learn to deal with your own strengths and weaknesses. Ray Allen knows how many practice shots he has to take and make to perform at the level he wants.

The closest thing we've experienced to this is doing stand-up comedy and business keynotes.

One of the ways Brian learned that his writing was stronger than his natural extroversion is that he's more likely to fail at stand-up (not get as many laughs, not feel like he enjoyed it, feel like the audience didn't enjoy it either) without spending a lot of time writing and preparing material before performing. He can do spontaneous, extroverted funny with others in the context of improv comedy scenes, but more reliably with improv games than in freeform long form improv. He requires a certain amount of structure.

Other performers seem more spontaneous. Some comedians talk about writing onstage. Brian hasn't had the guts to do that. He's actually funniest about an hour before he performs stand-up. In the glare of the lights, with the cortisol in his bloodstream, it's easy for him to lose his place.

This is one of the reasons he's so dependent on PowerPoint. It's his goal to move beyond this. But he's terrified of forgetting important points and losing track up on stage. Right now, PowerPoint is a crutch that ensures he can perform at a high level, because he has people to teach and entertain and meeting planners to satisfy. We think his reliance on this crutch will change in five or ten years.

When he first started doing stand-up, he did much more spontaneous crowdwork. It can work but it's not as reliable. Crowds love it for the same reason they love improv — it's being created right now. It's riskier. We want to see either a big failure or a big success. Todd Barry did a crowdwork-only tour, and you can buy the video on Louis C.K.'s site. It's awesome. There's always some amount of spontaneous in Brian's act and his keynotes, but for him it's 20%, not 80%.

You have to determine your own mix; what do you need to succeed?

Trial and error, baby. Figure it out.

## Opposition Makes Us Stronger

Without the Pistons "Bad Boys" and Stockton/Malone and Hakeem "The Dream" Olajuwon, His Aireness Michael Jordan might not have become the greatest of all time. Our enemies and obstacles give us the tests and the motivation to grow stronger.

Harry Potter series writer J.K. Rowling's cowbell is clearly writing fiction, perhaps specifically for young adults. The first 12 publishers rejected Rowling's first Harry Potter book. There are so many stories like that — successful books initially rejected. We look back at the success of

Harry Potter and cannot fathom who would be so stupid as to pass up that book. It's a lot like Decca Records passing on the Beatles, saying that "guitar groups are on the way out" and "the Beatles have no future in show business." Things like that seem so stupid to us.

But how much more stupid would it have been for Rowling or the Beatles to give up?

"There's nothing like a humiliating loss to focus the mind." – Phil Jackson

"It's only work if you'd rather be doing something else." – Pauline Phillips (better known as Dear Abby)

Obstacles Define Us

The challenges you face will reveal to you - and everyone else - who you are and what you really want. That obstacle in front of you is, in a sense, the world asking you, "How badly do you really want this?"

"We cannot solve our problems with the same thinking we used when we created them." — Albert Einstein

Sometimes the answer is to realize that you want something more than you thought you did. For some people — especially very competitive people — the realization comes quickly, spurring an almost immediate rally. Kobe Bryant is one of these competitive, resilient types. We can conclude that from his statement (earlier in this chapter) about viewing all challenges as opportunities.

His mindset is to spring back up when tripped by an obstacle. You can crawl out of failure and trudge toward success. Challenges in life are like weights. You can't get stronger without them. The power of your will cannot be exercised without obstacles. Strengthen your and you change your destiny.

## AMY MARLENE—CREATE LIKE AN ARTIST, THINK LIKE A BUSINESSWOMAN

Both baking and styling would have allowed Amy to express herself, but when she was hairstylist to Brian and his wife, they found that she had a gift for empathy and listening. As a baker, she would not get to use this gift nearly as much! Amy would never choose to feel exploited, but her reaction to that feeling led her to become a smarter businesswoman who now blends her creativity and empathy in a profitable, fulfilling way.

Amy's darkest times while trying to find her own cowbell almost led her into a different creative field. At times feeling like she was being taken advantage of, she persisted in the salon industry because she had a passion for interacting with clients. She overcame discouragement and learned how to succeed at what she loves. Here's her story…

When I graduated from high school, it was time to decide what I wanted to do with the rest of my life. Ha!

At the time, I had been studying health science and progressing in the beginning stages of the nursing field but, when it was time to enroll in college I announced to my mom and dad that I didn't want to wear booties and a hair net for the rest of my life (because that's what "they" said — the rest of my life). My parents supported my decision.

Beauty school was my alternative. I always enjoyed styling and the concept of hair color. I was known for being brave with my hair and highlighting my friends' hair in my parents' garage. At 18, I wasn't expecting the experience that unfolded to me as I became a professional in the industry. Here's kind of how it went:

<u>Me</u>: Mallory, we need to discuss what's going on with my pay. If I am salary, why is my paycheck all of a sudden different?

<u>Mallory</u>: Well, you will have to talk to Scott about that.

<u>Me</u>: No, Scott is not my boss. (Scott was the guy who ran the salon meetings for us out of the kindness of his heart. He just cared about all of us and wanted us to succeed. After I left, I found out he was the investor.)

<u>Mallory</u>: Well, I started charging you $5-$10 for every color client to make sure the color is paid for. The salon is spending too much money in color.

<u>Me</u>: That's not right, Mallory. In fact I'm really mad about this! How long has this extra color charge been going on and why didn't you discuss it with me?

That's it in a nutshell. You can only imagine all the other crap going on in a salon where a boss takes it upon herself to change your pay when salary was already a rip-off to begin with. I started out as commission; then they changed it to salary for their benefit and then still found ways to rip me off.

I wanted to be a baker for the creativity, but I also imagined working where I could interact with customers. I like treating people. In fact, a lot of nurses become hairstylists and vice versa because of the core similarities. Statistics say, anyway… but, for me, hairstyling is a better way for me to express myself.

What I enjoyed doing has turned into my passion over the last eight years. During this time, I have worked for people who have inspired me and those who took advantage of me. This led me to create as an artist and think as a businesswoman. When I worked for an employer who took advantage of me I thought about giving up in the salon industry and moving into the baking industry because I enjoyed baking. I thought to myself, baking pastries is creative and I will have the opportunity to offer people something special.

Instead, I found an opportunity to open my own salon with a colleague, and we ran it successfully for three years together. I now live in New York City working as a stylist at a high-end boutique hair studio. I love what I do and I allowed my heart to lead the way. I am able to create, which in my opinion is a very important part of being human. I'm able to generate money for my hard work and talents. I feel it is an energetic exchange between working, creating, and compensation.

## MARK WHITNEY—REVENGE, THE ULTIMATE MOTIVATOR

What pisses you off so much you would do anything to fix it?

In 1987, I gave two tax returns to three banks that were not quite what they appeared to be and the judge gave me a three-year timeout. On Jan. 10, 1992, I hugged my wife and sons goodbye and reported to federal prison, where I immediately went to work on securing my freedom. A mere 452 days later, then-Chief Judge for the U.S. Court of Appeals for the First Circuit (not Supreme Court Justice) Stephen G. Breyer declared my term of imprisonment unconstitutional, ordering my immediate release.

Within five minutes I was escorted to the edge of the compound. They gave me two weeks' pay — a roll of dimes — and I walked my first mile out of federal prison. I came up on the White Deer Motel and said to the people there, "You're not going to believe this. I just got thrown out of jail!"

They let me call my wife, who knew it was good news because it wasn't collect. Julie, Chris, and Michael drove the nine hours from Vermont to Pennsylvania: "Let's run, Dad!"

And we did. We ran until we couldn't run anymore.

Ninety-nine percent of appeals fail. I am a high school graduate. I represented myself. I didn't win that appeal because of anything having to do with the law. I won that appeal because I wanted to be free more than the government wanted me in prison. The government has vast resources. But they made the mistake of giving me the time to outwork them.

The litigation started in 1988 with a Chapter 11 petition and ended a decade later when I successfully negotiated a $20,000 settlement with the IRS; about four cents on the dollar. Shortly thereafter, I started TheLaw.net Corporation (TLN). Today more than 500,000 lawyers pay to use the syndicated, searchable database of six million judicial opinions.

If I learned one thing as a result of these experiences, it was that lawyers for the Department of Justice could see all the law via very expensive databases built by West and Lexis.

TLN levels the playing field by providing all the law to any attorney for $50 a month. As much as I was driven to build a company with a passive income stream that would support my family while allowing me to speak and write about civil liberties, I wanted West and Lexis and their institutional subscribers to suffer.

Eighty hours a week in a prison law library for 15 months was all it took to restore order for my family. TLN brought order to the formerly chaotic, unfair situation plaguing small law offices.

Customers say things like "This is the best damn research program I have ever seen in 40 years of practicing law. I just love it!"

Become the world's leading expert on something — anything. And never underestimate the value of a chip on your shoulder.

**How To Put Chapter Four Into Action And Get The Results You Want**

- Make a list of people who've disliked you or criticized you or blocked you.

o Did they teach you anything?

o Did it help you do your cowbell in a better way?

o Use opposition to motivate yourself- next to each of your critics, write down what you're going to do or achieve to "show them". Now make it happen.

- Is there something you're afraid your peers or competitors would say negatively about you- even if they don't?

o Is that criticism valid something you should work on?

- Go to LinkedIn and ask for profile recommendations from people you've helped.

- Make sure your bio contains all your achievements and credibility markers.

- If you're really having trouble with confidence, work on your bio and recommendations. Make the most of what you have. Make sure there's something people can relate to in it. Read your accomplishments out loud to yourself.

**Hey You, Did You Get Your Free Cowbell Principle Bonuses?**
As the owner of this book (even if you somehow got it for free) you are entitled to some awesome bonuses!

> **#1.** The controversial chapter they made us take out! "True Secrets of Success That Make People Uncomfortable" You may not want to read this one... it's very unconventional. But it's all so true that it's funny. And if you're the kind of person that just wishes people would level with you, you'll love it!

> **#2.** The Superfun Cowbell Overview Webinar

> **#3.** Mystery bonus! Better than mystery meat, guaranteed!

> To get them, go to http://thecowbellprinciple.com/bonuses and opt in!

# 5. Testing: You Never Know What's Going to Click

"You never know what's going to click," said Christopher Walken in real life when he first was told how popular the "More Cowbell" sketch had become. Think about it: Christopher Walken is one of the most frequent Saturday Night Live guests ever. He's done more than 50 monologues and sketches. "More Cowbell" clearly wasn't the one he thought was the best.

It's that way in life and business. You never know what's really going to resonate with people. You have to try a bunch of stuff to find those few great things.

Malcolm Gladwell popularized Anders Ericsson's research that it requires 10,000 hours of practice to become a master at anything. But practice doesn't make perfect. Perfect practice makes perfect. Say you're a basketball player —instead of making it a goal to shoot 800 shots before you stop, make it a goal to make 800 shots before you stop, like Kobe Bryant has. Accept only perfect practice.

John Hayes, a cognitive psychology professor at Carnegie Mellon University, analyzed thousands of musical pieces produced between the years of 1685 and 1900. The central question that drove his work was "How long after one becomes interested in music is it that one becomes world class?" What he discovered was that virtually every single "masterwork" was written after year 10 of the composer's career. Out of 500 pieces there were only three exceptions, which were written in years eight and nine.

So what?

The upshot is this: If you find your cowbell, and the income from its practice fuels you enough to keep going indefinitely, then eventually you will produce something great.

The Cowbell Principle is not "find your passion and your life will immediately be awesome." Life just doesn't work that way for most people. A lot of hard work and a few lucky breaks, though, can create a happy and successful career. And of course, the harder you work, the more luck you seem to have. So focus on the work.

## Science vs. Stubbornness

Scientific research is conducted to try to discover facts. We want to separate opinion and other factors from what we know. The goal is to be sure that what we think we know is really true. So, believe it or not, researchers have conducted research on the topic of research. They've discovered more than 50 biases (incorrect assumptions) that affect how people do research and how they interpret it. For example, a study of physicians reading research found that MDs were much more likely to question a study's methodology if they disagreed with the conclusions. Turns out we ask fewer questions when we hear confirmation of what we already believe.

What do many geniuses do daily that would blow most people's minds? They enjoy changing their minds, something that a lot of people hate to do. Why? They aren't focused on looking good. They're focused on good results.

Robert Cialdini, a psychology and marketing professor and author, wrote a landmark book called Influence: The Psychology of Persuasion. He wrote about six key principles of influence, one of which is Commitment, or Consistency. Once people say something, or publicly commit to it, they tend to stick to it. We can be stubborn in trying to protect our reputation. But this tendency fights against new discoveries. What if we were wrong? You may have to fight yourself in order to give yourself permission to change your mind.

What happens when normal people gives themselves permission to be wrong? They move forward and succeed faster. Do you want to be right or do you want to win? It's really okay to change your mind. If anyone questions you, ask, "Would you really think me smarter or more respectable for sticking up for an error?"

## Science vs. Inspiration

U.S. companies spend over $6 billion each year on market research. Globally, market research may be as much as an $18 billion annual investment. This seems like a smart and responsible activity, because companies want to be sure that they're serving the customer and that people want what they're producing.

But science only goes so far without inspiration.

Steve Jobs said something contrary here, because the iPhone didn't come from market research. It came from creative inspiration. Jobs said, "People don't know what they want until you show it to them."

Brian's experience testing hundreds of blog posts and thousands of advertisements and social media posts confirms this. You can analyze data and poll users, and this will lead to better results overall, but often the most successful ideas — those dramatic outliers that outperform all your others — come straight from inspiration. You're not really sure how you thought of it.

Garrison's anonymous interviews with top performers over 10 years (with some help from Gallup) had similar results. The top 1% of the 5,371 people interviewed did things that were beyond just better results. They often were not sure how they came up with their market-dominating ideas. And many were inspired by some pretty simple stuff. The founder of a large rental company with minimal education said, "It dawned on me one day that millions of people wanted basic stuff they could never afford. So I thought, 'Well, heck, I can rent stuff like couches, tables, and stereo systems.' I couldn't get a single partner because people thought it was such a horrible idea. So I invented the industry and pretty much made all the money, and now everybody thinks I'm a genius!"

After years of poring over customer data regarding why they didn't buy something they said they loved, wanted, and needed, the Rental King discovered a simple cultural fact: Many people who can't afford to buy the American dream are willing to rent it.

The role of science is to confirm and improve what you're doing. Knowing the facts of your niche and data about your customers will help you have better ideas. Those inspired ideas need to be tracked. The data will tell you which of them was best and will guide you in the future.

So, you have to test. You have to track. And you have to be creative.

Throw a bunch of stuff at the wall and see what sticks, shotgun-style.

Really? Aren't we smart enough not to need a shotgun? No, research shows that even advertisers with decades of experience can't predict what will or won't work any better than newbies can.

One way to look at the history of culture is millions of people throwing stuff at the wall and most of it not sticking. Viral, super-good stuff is rare, but that's what endures.

Come up with more ideas. Keep testing. You never know where that great idea's going to come from.

When you're stuck, answer these questions:

- Who and what are you ignoring?
- What are you assuming that maybe you shouldn't?
- Who can you talk to about your work?
- Where else can you look for ideas?
- What ideas can you take from one realm into your niche?

You never know where that great idea's going to come from.

Bruce Dickinson said, "Really explore the studio space this time. I mean really. Explore the space." Focus and go for the feel. Intuitive creation. Let go.

There is no judgment allowed during creation. Stop analyzing. No worry or fear. The creation place and process must be protected like a baby in the womb. Be gentle with it.

You never know what's going to click.

## ERIK QUALMAN — AUTHOR WHO BET ON HIMSELF

Called a Digital Dale Carnegie, Erik Qualman was voted the 2nd Most Likeable Author in the World behind Harry Potter's J.K. Rowling. Fast Company ranks him as a Top 100 Digital Influencer and PC Magazine lists his blog as a Top 10 Social Media blog. A frequently requested international keynote speaker (42 countries), he has been featured on almost every media outlet including 60 Minutes, The Wall Street Journal, and ABC News. He is listed as a Top 50 MBA Professor and is no stranger to the executive suite, having served as the Head of Marketing at Travelzoo®; today he sits on several company boards. Yet, he may be best known for writing and producing the world's most watched social media video. Socialnomics was a finalist for the "Book of the Year." Qualman was Academic All-Big Ten in basketball at Michigan State University and Erik was honored as the Michigan State University Alum of the Year. He also holds a Guinness Book of World Record for the longest continuous podcast. Here's his story…

I didn't know whether to cry or scream, so I did both. The lifetime savings I'd carefully cultivated over a 17-year career had vanished in a Ponzi scheme. Half a million dollars was gone and it wasn't coming back. The fact that friends of mine who were CFOs or worked for the major investment banks had also been hoodwinked in the same scheme was of little consolation. Unlike them, this was my entire savings.

It turned out to be the best $500,000 education of my life. It taught me:

1.     Your money can be washed away in a second, so you might as well do something you love. Tim Ferriss talks a lot about this principle in his book The 4-Hour Workweek.

2.     Bet on yourself.

But I'm getting ahead of myself. Back to the story on how I came to these two guiding principles.

After realizing the money was gone, the next few days were rough. Questions bounced around in my head, but the recurring question was, "Now what?" To help get out of my funk, I started asking my closest friends and colleagues, "What do you think I do well?" Their positive answers helped lift my spirits, but they also helped give me clarity regarding my strengths. The answers were consistent. People consistently indicated that I was really good at three things:

1.     Seeing big digital trends before they were popular.

2.     Being able to explain difficult digital concepts in an easy and fun way.

3.     Interacting with people — I feel that everyone has a story to tell and a nice gift is to allow them to tell it by listening.

One person's insight hit me squarely in the face: "Erik, I don't know why you were so stupid to lose all that money betting on someone else. If I had your talents, I'd bet on myself." Then another friend of mine, an author, suggested, "You should write a book on the digital trends you always talk about. I can get you in contact with my publisher."

I decided to take the leap and do both. Most importantly, I was going to bet on myself. This was a difficult decision, as I had a great job that I liked and I also had a wife and two little girls to support. This wasn't the time to bet on myself! I needed a stable job for the next 17 years to earn back the money I lost. However, what lesson would I be teaching my kids if I didn't bet on myself?

So off to New York I went to meet with the publisher. Now, keep in mind I had finished a fiction novel several years prior that never saw the light of day. In my drawer were stuffed over one thousand rejection letters from publishers and agents. This was back when they would send you paper instead of an email. I saved the letters as motivation, but how would this time be different? Well, at least the meeting was face-to-face — and since this was an identified strength, perhaps I had a chance.

The day before the meeting, I needed to figure out a title for my nonfiction book. After brainstorming for a few hours, I came up with the title Socialnomics: How Social Media Will Change the Way We Live and Do Business. I googled "socialnomics" and it came back with zero results. Yes! This would be my title (even though I had no clue how to fill out the forms I filed online that day for the trademark for Socialnomics).

The meeting went well and I was awarded a contract. I quickly wrote the book and, since I talked a lot about YouTube in the book, I also decided that I should launch the book with a YouTube video. The book became a No. 1 bestseller in seven languages. And the video I produced for $300 is still the most watched video about social media on YouTube. Today if you google "Socialnomics" you'll get over a quarter-million results.

The book and video were my springboard. There was no looking back. What did I get for betting on my strengths?

- Three international bestsellers and counting
- Voted the second most likeable author in the world behind Harry Potter's J.K. Rowling
- Guinness Book of World Records member
- Have given keynotes in 42 countries for the likes of IBM, United Healthcare, Sony, Chrysler, Starbucks, National Guard, M&M-Mars, and more
- Have a booming studio in Equalman Studios whose video clients include the likes of Disney, Cartier, and Chase
- Have shared the stage with Al Gore, Julie Andrews, Magic Johnson, Malcolm Gladwell, Bill O'Reilly, Jeff Bezos, Howard Schultz, Brett Favre, Tony Hawk, Sarah Palin, Condoleezza Rice, Alan Mulally, and many others of note

Looking back, losing the $500,000 was just the shock I needed to go from being a wantrapreneur (credit: Mark Cuban) to being an entrepreneur. I love what I do. I run my own business in Equalman Studios, and I get paid to travel the world, meeting great people and companies, primarily teaching them about digital leadership, digital reputation, and trends and innovation.

The happy ending to this story is that in my first year of business I made back the 17 years' worth of savings I lost.

While this was an expensive education, my hope is that I have now given you the same education, for FREE. Bet on your strengths today. After all, this is how I became known as the Digital Dale Carnegie.

## JEFF WIDMAN — LASER-FOCUSED PROBLEM-SOLVING

Jeff Widman has built and sold two companies, and advised brands like Microsoft, Intel and the Washington Redskins. He's been quoted as an expert on Facebook marketing by the Wall Street Journal, Advertising Age, CNN, Adweek, Mashable, Wired, TechCrunch, Fortune, TheNextWeb, etc. He was the outside consultant who advised YouTube how to become the fastest growing Facebook page in the world. He has an insatiable appetite for beating the system by doing things a little differently. To decompress, he heads outdoors. He's biked a century, run a marathon without training, and backpacked 50 miles in 24 hours. Jeff is passionate about: efficiency, technology and metrics-based marketing. Here's his story…

My cowbell is focused analytical problem solving. I'm an obsessive scientist. I cofounded PageLever, a company that provided Facebook marketing analytics for business. We had a successful exit by selling PageLever to Unified.

With PageLever, we started with the features people really wanted. For example, social media managers wanted alerts when a post really took off; they also wanted emailed reports. We were successful in part because we had shifted from running a large agency helping brands with Facebook. We built software to solve our own problems. We laid out five major things we wanted to achieve or offer, which turned out to be the core things our audience liked. We understood the space really well.

Before long, PageLever had an advantage because we had access to everybody's data. We aggregated it all and got averages. It was anonymous and private, but it allowed us to report to customers and media how the average page was doing: "I thought I was doing poorly but I'm doing well compared to others," or vice versa. That was our hook; media came to us and asked how companies were performing on Facebook and what people on Facebook were doing. We knew more than anyone else in the space. We had technical developers to support the marketing. There were no silos in our way.

Other tech companies weren't solving the right problems. And some marketers didn't have the data they needed. Our product advantage was we were practitioners. Our marketing advantage was our data.

We got so many users in the beginning because we've worked with some big brands: YouTube, Microsoft, and Intel. We had data from the beginning.

Before PageLever, I was running the agency when a company approached us about buying us out. My fiancée (now my wife) and I reviewed the offer but decided not to sell to them. My fiancée said, "Look, Jeff, you'll make more money but they'll want you to work a ton of hours."

We were just getting married. I told my team, "Guys, this company can pay you more; you should go join that team." Instead, one team member wanted to work with me, so we cofounded PageLever. The idea of making more money was appealing but we made a lifestyle decision away from that.

Of course, PageLever took more and more of my time, and now my wife is clear she doesn't want me to do another PageLever!

We eventually sold for a couple reasons. We reached a point where we anticipated that the market would continue to shift quickly, making it necessary for us to be part of a suite of products; customers wanted us to do a little of everything to be a one-stop shop. We'd have to raise a lot of money or sell.

I was struggling. I was a good individual contributor but not a good manager. I wouldn't be able to go the distance. My partner David was doing a great job leveling up but I wasn't. It was undermining my self-confidence. So we said, "Let's de-risk, join forces, get cash and stock."

The experience taught me my strengths and weaknesses.

My real strength is focus. When I really dive into a problem, I'm myopic; I research and think about the problem and I don't care about doing something the same way as everybody else.

In the early days of Facebook, when everybody was into custom tabs, I questioned what users were really doing. They weren't going to tabs. They were in the newsfeed! You want a snazzy tab to impress the boss? It flew in the face of all conventional wisdom. It wasn't courage — I just didn't care what other experts thought. I had the tenacity to look for facts and find ways to improve.

When we launched PageLever, we had a landing page that said these big-name companies are using this tool to get more fans, more engagement, and more traffic. When people entered their info, we asked them to "share" if they wanted into the beta sooner. I realized they could give us more exposure if we asked for it. So we got a lot more traffic and users early. I'm great at that kind of problem solving.

But I'm bad at quick decisions or doing just good enough. I don't like management because good managers can't get stuck in actual work. They have to empower and coach. They give their employees resources. What I like is to be curious and dig into things. I'm obsessed with doing it better, not doing it just good enough.

It's a low-prestige activity. Prestigious is to run and manage a big company, but I don't have the inclination. It's really humbling to do what I'm really best at.

I think personalization is something marketers will be working on for the next 50 years.

## NICK UNSWORTH — 10 FAILURES BEFORE SUCCESS

Nick Unsworth is a Social Media Pro who teaches entrepreneurs, business owners, and service professionals how to build a tribe of raving fans, followers, and customers that will grow their brand and bottom line. Here's his story...

My cowbell is helping people find their purpose. My business is Life On Fire.

I wrote a letter to myself at age 25 about what my life would be like at 30. What I saw was I wanted to help people and give to charity.

As a business coach, I serve clients who pay me for strategy and for figuring out how to monetize their purpose. If they don't have that purpose, they're usually stuck doing something they're not good at. They're not excelling; they're not in the zone because there's not enough meaning attached to what they're doing.

Once they have that greater purpose and meaning, everything falls into place. They can't be stopped. Challenges that would have been mountains become anthills.

I had this awareness that I really wanted to figure out my purpose, but it took me 12 years to get into my groove.

My dad had a really stressful life as a commercial builder. Work consumed him. He would drive from Connecticut to New Hampshire, two and a half hours each way. He wasn't around. I definitely thought he didn't like his job. In response, I wanted to love what I did. I didn't want to work for other people. I saw how the company cut my dad and granddad's pensions.

I did what I thought was best for me. I took an internship with a top 10 financial firm. I learned about residual income and referral-based businesses. But selling insurance wasn't that exciting.

So I was just trying to turn enough stones to find my thing. I couldn't answer, "What is my purpose?" I didn't have any mentorships for that. No Bruce Dickinson. I had to fail forward. I had to try on many pairs of shoes to see what fit.

I got into network marketing. I enjoyed building a big team. I really thought that was my purpose. I was on cloud nine every day. But I realized I was doing well but my team below me wasn't duplicating my success. It's a brutal industry. People came in and spent money but didn't make any. I realized I wasn't helping people.

I got into real estate at the wrong time, around 2005. I was really just chasing money. I was young; I thought if I made a lot, I could give a lot back. But I hated real estate and didn't make that much money.

Next, I had a nonprofit that failed. It was like a Groupon for the local market. We raised money for charity as part of it. My parents and friends thought I had hit it. But a trademark infringement led to failure. It was called the New Perks Card. It gave local discounts to 45 locations. Cardholders would get 50% off a bottle of wine, 10% off at a grocery, and 20% off at a dry cleaner. It cost $20 and $10 of that went to charity. We forced the buyers to choose which charity. We thought that forcing them to choose would open their eyes to care more about giving. At the same time, I was a realtor so I was getting my name out there. I got on TV and in the papers.

I was doing so well that I wanted to take it to the next level, so I contacted an ad agency. They were pushing TV commercials at me and telling me they had 100 years of combined experience. They said, "You have to do TV commercials." I didn't trust my gut, which was saying to do online instead. The ad guys said the 6 p.m. news was the best spot. It was broadcast to all of Connecticut. But I said, "We're only talking about local discounts. Who would drive two hours for this?" It defied logic but I put my faith in them.

I contracted for $40,000, which was literally everything I had and then some on credit cards. Ten thousand dollars went to production and then the ad spend was $10,000 a week.

The commercials aired and we got obscene amounts of web traffic, but no one bought anything. We spent $10,000 in that first week and sold two cards. It destroyed me; I'd burned all my cash and we didn't sell cards. So I pulled the plug.

Then I got this big packet in the mail. It was a notice to cease and desist from a Chicago law firm threatening me with a lawsuit. When I called, they wanted to talk to my lawyer. I said, "I'm 23. I don't have any money and I don't have a lawyer." I became my own attorney.

Apparently, New Perks Card was confusingly similar to their name. I had wanted to trademark before we started, but people advised me not to. I had a real estate attorney do the trademark name search but he screwed it up.

Meanwhile, we were still getting more traffic to the website, so I called the ad guys and said, "We aren't still running ads, are we?" They said no, we were done with the ads. "Then how are we getting all this traffic?" I asked.

I found out that we ranked on first page of Google for "perks card." And the lawsuit was really because of the traffic we took from the other company.

What I learned out of all that was that traditional marketing doesn't work. Then the ad reps explained, "You don't expect ads to make you money." I said, "How does that make any sense at all?"

So I switched it up again. I got into Facebook marketing. I wanted people to make money, not lose it.

I sold my business, which had been my dream my whole life. My girlfriend and I broke up and I moved to San Diego. I'm sitting there beachfront and feeling emotionally devastated, alone, dead inside. This wasn't what I expected. Then I got a personal development coach, because I thought "I should be really happy but I'm not." It wasn't about money. I wanted to be happy, help people, and have a life with meaning behind it.

My "Aha!" moment was the realization that I was always chasing shiny-object opportunities. I learned this through my business coach's exercises, where I'd be asked to explore things like "What pisses you off?" and "What's your movement?" I got back to how my dad lived, with no time for his kids. I knew I wanted to be a dad, have kids, and be around for them. But I was clearly a workaholic; to sell a business, I had sacrificed my entire 20s.

Everyone is full of this BS that being an entrepreneur is so glorious, but most of my entrepreneur friends have less quality of life than the people who work in corporate America. I wanted to live a life on fire, to love what I do every day. Working takes up most of our time, so why not love it? Why not impact lives? Do it in an enjoyable way.

Now, I don't do tasks I don't like. I help people figure out what their purpose is: What's the right lifestyle and business model? Don't just gun for the destination.

If you look back, several times I thought I'd found my purpose, but I was wrong. There is a shortcut to avoid some of that. That's what I do with my coaching; I get people there faster. I can take a stranger and get him damn close in 30 minutes. I also do half a day and I'm 10 for 10 with elite clients. I can get them super clear but they still have to execute and then re-evaluate. They have to go from a scatterbrained entrepreneur to someone with focused purpose.

Trial and error is normal. I ask people, "If you could have the lifestyle you want, if you could be happy and fulfilled, but you knew you had to fail at x businesses to get it — and you don't know how many failures that is… my number was 11! — would you still want it bad enough to go after it?"

The people I help? Those who have a fever for my cowbell? They want more. They know they're not doing what they love. They're not happy or fulfilled (which is 95% of the population).

I love podcasting and Facebook marketing, because it's such a good way to build a lifestyle business. For example, two of my mentees were foster kids, an aspect of their background that actually helps them connect with people. They can interview entrepreneurs who were foster kids — people they couldn't otherwise get onto their show — because they share that same wound.

Your wound can create your purpose and give you a competitive advantage.

Take what you're good at, get clear on your passion and purpose, and help people love what they do.

**How To Put Chapter Five Into Action And Get The Results You Want**

- Create Facebook Ads to test your ideas- business ideas, slogans, business names, etc.

o Which ones have the highest click through rates? These are the ones people are most interested in.

- Create a survey with SurveyMonkey.com and ask your peers just one key open-ended question (can't be answered with just yes or no)- example questions:

o What do you think my unique talent is?

o What problems have you seen me solve best?

o If I could do one thing to take my career to the next level, what would it be? Allow this survey to be taken anonymously.

**Hey You, Did You Get Your Free Cowbell Principle Bonuses?**
As the owner of this book (even if you somehow got it for free) you are entitled to some awesome bonuses!

**#1.** The controversial chapter they made us take out! "True Secrets of Success That Make People Uncomfortable" You may not want to read this one... it's very unconventional. But it's all so true that it's funny. And if you're the kind of person that just wishes people would level with you, you'll love it!

**#2.** The Superfun Cowbell Overview Webinar

**#3.** Mystery BONUS! Better than mystery meat, guaranteed.

To get your free bonuses, go to thecowbellprinciple.com/bonuses and opt the heck in!

# 6. Teamwork: The Perfect Team Is Not Perfect

It's awesome to have a group of peers. You could have your own Blue Öyster Cult! Yes, that's the band from the sketch. It's proof that obscurity was an essential part of their DNA that they are the focus of one of the most famous SNL sketches ever, but still not more famous for it.

Your group will not always be right, but they'll still be awesome.

Community is one of those words so overused that you wonder if it still means anything. But a guy playing a cowbell by himself is insane… and possibly trying to collect some money on the street.

You never see anybody seesawing by himself (we hope). For the same reason, a cowbell requires someone else. It has to be played within an ensemble. Honestly, nobody wants to hear a cowbell solo. Someday there might arise a Jimi Hendrix of the cowbell, but to achieve that level of "artistry," he'd have to be on even more drugs than Hendrix — and to enjoy it, so would we!

If your cowbell isn't helping anyone else, it's probably just an experiment in psychotic selfishness.

A cowbell has to add something. It has to make a contribution. Your cowbell should allow you to be part of a community. It gives you a role to play. The cowbell is rhythmic, but often that beat is established by the drummer. Do you understand how your cowbell fits in with others?

It's important that your cowbell meshes within a community. In the sketch, the cowbell had to fit in. In fact, that was the source of most of the conflict.

Because a cowbell adds value to your community, it makes you an important part of that community. You may not be accepted at first; but stand up for your unique contribution, and others will acknowledge your value.

When Brian or Garrison speaks, the meeting or conference might go on for eight hours or even for days. The speaker is not the only focus. He's part of the process — a necessary part, but only a part. The speaker has to learn what conference is about, what the other speakers are going to talk about, and what the goals and theme of the conference are. Why is the audience there? Why do the audience members think they're there? What big issues are they working on? What big changes have happened and how have they affected the group? When speakers discover those answers, they can make a bigger contribution and become part of that community of being successful together.

So, how do you get your cowbell to fit into the community that needs it? There can be conflict in the process of fitting in, but everyone needs to figure out the best fit.

You might need to have the willingness to say, "My cowbell as it is might not fit here. How can I make it fit?" New employees often go through this. What's important to everybody else? You get trained. You get the lay of the land. You learn the power structure. You learn that you can't say certain things to certain people. You learn which of the things you want to do might make it seem like you're stepping on somebody else's toes. Adjust yourself to fit in.

People skills, diplomacy, and being helpful are critical for successful teamwork. If you don't handle people well, your cowbell can rub them the wrong way, and then it's not valued. Your behavior can eclipse your skill. A ton of people are fired every year despite their skills.

There's a lot of talk in last 30 years about how to be an individual. We tell kids, "You don't have to fit in. Be yourself. You're good as is!" Absolutely you should be yourself, unless you're a psychotic jerk. Then don't be yourself. Try to be a nicer person, instead.

You can't be part of community if the community believes you're not making a contribution. You can't be so different that they can't relate to you. If you can't adapt, you might need to find a different community. There's nothing wrong with finding out you belong somewhere else.

Are you flexible enough to make adjustments along the way to reach the goal — both your goals and the team's? In marriage, it's not necessarily a 50-50 arrangement; maybe your spouse simply can't change certain things and you should adapt to that.

An important part of being influential is listening. Make sure people feel heard, listened to, and cared for. If people feel that way, they'll see you as a good fit. People accept you if they feel heard and listened to and valued.

Have you ever met anybody who's a real character? These people are unique but we love them. We let them get away with more than we do the people we don't like. If you don't like someone, you can just suspect they did something, and you feel like you have cause to act (or speak) against them.

Why do we trust real characters? We know they're being who they are, so we'll let them get away with more. With a shrug and a grin, we might explain, "The laptops? Oh, yeah, ol' Jimmy just stole some... He'll bring 'em back. You know Jimmy!" Now, this section is not written to demonize people name Jimmy, but our research shows that people named Jimmy tend to have a lot of trouble — Jimmy Carter, for instance... to whom Brian is not related.

We all know a Jimmy type, don't we? And their character is consistent.

People trust consistency. If you're the same person in front of family, friends, loved ones, and coworkers, then you're consistent.

It's common for some guy to get promoted and suddenly be managing people who last week were his peers. Sometimes the new manager puts on a leadership mask, which creates a problem. He dresses and acts differently. People wonder what the heck's going on, and it kills the trust they used to have with that person. "That ol' Jimmy's putting on airs now!" You're not trusted as much anymore. You don't fit in and you don't have as much influence, especially if your name is Jimmy. Resist the temptation to be someone else. Be you. Be consistently you! You have authority now by virtue of your new position. Explain what's going on and you'll be good.

The hardest change for people to accept is a change in a person. We love to say that people don't change, but they do. That's one reason marriages fail. You might not see who you married anymore, they've changed so much. People lose trust. Women complain that men make money and become successful and change. A lot of people don't deal well with fame (even microfame) or success.

So, how can you relate to people more effectively?

• Listen and make people feel valuable.
• Clearly explain the value of what you have to offer.
• Make sure people can see their input in your solution.
• Ask questions. Find out what they think and want.
• Know what's important to them. What are their goals?

People who like you will adapt to you. And you can adapt to people you understand.

We're not suggesting you make such radical, "community-approved" changes that your cowbell no longer resembles your cowbell. But if you can make subtle changes that enable your cowbell to intermesh better, you build stronger community for your cowbell. Community feels more tied to it/invested in it

Pro quarterbacks come onto a new team and are often released in four months. Sometimes that's because they have their own way of doing things that doesn't fit with the new team. Garrison went from playing public high school football to private. He found the new team had a completely different playbook. He could try to make improvements to what they were doing, but he also had to accept their way of doing it. In real situations, change can cause more trouble than the theoretical benefit of the change itself. Small changes, if accepted, can create real improvement. But people don't accept change from someone who doesn't care about them. Try to understand and listen to them, and they'll make changes for you.

To that end, Garrison developed a process called Ask – Listen – Agree – Recommend.

- Ask a question.
- Listen as they answer.
- Let them know that you agree.
- Recommend something that includes their input.

People love to hear their ideas in your solution. The things people say are the things they believe in and are committed to. Agreement is a critical step, because people hold on so tightly to their beliefs and commitments.

The foundation of true agreement is disagreement. Let people be honest and put their cards on the table. Try to find out where you all agree. What can we all commit to, since we're not on the same page? Look for middle ground that's effective. It's not about everybody contributing one weird piece, because that's how you get a Frankenstein that won't survive or thrive.

Want loyalty from your team? A person on a team in which members are allowed to disagree will be loyal to that team. Unfortunately, sometimes people mistake disagreement for disloyalty. Yet, it's often observed that families whose members complain a lot are paradoxically loyal to each other, whereas families that don't express how they feel are disloyal and dysfunctional. To build a strong team and community, everyone must be allowed to not agree.

And the sense of unity that comes from disagreement is exactly what you see in the "More Cowbell" sketch.

## Not Looking for Homogeneity

That homogenous quality we look for in our dairy products is not what we ought to be looking for in our cowbell community. Having too much of the same thing, through and through, brings none of the deeper insight and benefits you get from diversity. In fact, as our chapter title points out, the perfect team is decidedly not perfect. If everybody on the team were the same, it wouldn't work. You need at least three types: the visionary, the butt kisser, and the negative guy.

- Visionary: "I see the future." This big-picture person dreams up direction and gives it shape.
- Butt kisser: "I see what you're seeing and it's beautiful!" Visionaries like consistent support and agreement. The butt kisser gets promoted because the visionary —and the team as a whole —needs him. It seems like a strong team where you have people on it who believe in what the team's doing.
- Negative guy: "I see every problem we're ever going to have before we have it (...and I can tell ya we're gonna die!)" Without negative people, we're blindsided. As long as you don't fire all these people for being negative, you have a built-in warning system.

A weird thing about teamwork is that the guy who went out to fight the saber-toothed tiger or the mastodon by himself is not our ancestor; that guy died pretty quickly. They were too much for one person to take down. The guy who said, "I'd better get more people... and more spears!" — That guy's our ancestor. Teamwork is the foundation of civilization. We've got to support each other. We survived because of our teamwork.

We're naturally designed to work together, so let's embrace it.

## The Cowbells and Teamwork of World War II

During World War II, there was no way for one country to win. The war was too spread out. No single country had all the ingredients to be successful.

The U.S. had no presence in Germany. We didn't understand their history. We didn't understand why they thought they should have more land in Europe. They were at war with Britain, who could not have survived if the Germans had invaded physically. The U.S. didn't have enough pilots, so we secured Canadian pilots. It took effort from several nations. So what was each country's cowbell?

• America's manufacturing power was one of its cowbells in WWII. We didn't have to have superior tanks or soldiers because we had so many of them. There were more warships floating off the coast of Normandy when we invaded than Germany ever built. We also did well with our supply chain.

• The British had an attitude only they possess, which is "By virtue of who we are, we will never surrender. You'll have to kill all of us to win. We will not be occupied." Churchill said it (maybe not in those exact words) and everyone was on board.

• The French had wine, which didn't help very much. But seriously, the French underground helped.

Even the Germans had to make pacts with Japan and Russia. You can't do anything without allies and advocates.

### A Close Group of Peers: Who Is Your Blue Öyster Cult?

Sometimes the group's collective intelligence is best. If you can get into a productive, creative relationship with people, you get amazing things. The Beatles were better than solo John Lennon or solo Paul McCartney. And when that group creative thing works, it doesn't matter who came up with it. (But do have your contracts in place.)

You can be a small part of larger offerings. When were you a role player?

### DEREK COBURN— MUTUALLY BENEFICIAL NETWORKING

Derek is the co-founder of Cadre, an elite D.C. networking group. He wrote Networking Is Not Working, which is one of the top-selling business books on Amazon right now. Here's his story...

I found that my approach to networking is the ultimate tiebreaker. My clients don't jump ship easily. I had a client who was not fazed by someone who claimed to do the same service I do — and who claimed to do it better! I had referred this client $2 million of business while working for him. My value to him was much higher than just what I do professionally, so he wasn't too interested in switching.

Growing up, in middle school and high school, I didn't fit in. I tried to be somebody I wasn't to please others, to impress them, to make them like me. It didn't work for me or them. So I decided to be myself.

My cowbell is being a connector. I resisted saying that for years because so many people say "I'm a connector!" In fact, a lot of the "connector" emails frustrate me. A good 80-90% of the time when someone introduces me to someone else via email, there's no context or reason stated. It's better than nothing, but do you really think we're going to hit it off? Why are you connecting us? Should I research this person? Why? If the other connected person doesn't go first, I don't respond. And I'll bet there are "connectors" like this who say to themselves, "Whenever I try to connect people, it never goes anywhere!" Maybe the problem lies in how you do it.

I focus on mutually beneficial connections.

I attract high-level people because I know they need to get value out of relationships. Also, I help people I like and respect, without any expectation of getting anything back.

I'm friends with DeMaurice Smith (the head of the NFL Players Association), Chris Brogan, and the president of the only energy company in D.C. I don't identify people I want to get something out of. And I don't just give to everybody. I connect with people who are in my world, playing the same space, or who have the same mindset, interests, and other things in common. Then I figure out how to add value to them.

When I met John Dumas, who does the Entrepreneur on Fire podcast, immediately afterward I sent him four names of people I knew that he should have on his show. I said, "If you agree, I'll make introductions." It was good for his show and it got those people some exposure. Then he realized he wanted to get me on the show too. That's how it comes back to help you, but that's not why I do it.

My mindset is this: I'm always looking for ways I can create mutual value in my network.

People see me as a possible entree to the high-level people I associate with. But I have to protect those relationships. People ask, "Can you introduce me to X to get on his radar?" That may be the old way to network — and it may still be the norm in some niches. But it's outdated.

If I connect two people, I know why it makes sense for both of them. So when someone asks me for an introduction to a high-level person, I challenge the seeker. And actually that helps them, because it increases their chances of having a good relationship with those people. Even if I really like the person asking me, if I did that every time I would hurt my relationships with the VIPs. So, what's in it for them? Figure out the value you bring. If I know they're both going to be at Cadre, I'll say, "Grab me and I'll introduce you guys."

When it was time to put out my book, I felt I could ask for help on that. That was because I don't feel like I've directly asked for help from people — ever, maybe.

I get five to ten emails a week in which people ask, "Do you know a good x? Who do you recommend for y?" I got one that said, "We don't like working with recruiting firms. Do you know a salesperson?" I do know someone who's great at that. She has a five-person sales recruiter shop. I let her see the email. She saw that they're not keen on recruiting firms and told me, "These aren't the best potential clients for me." If I had introduced them and she wasted time before finding out they didn't like recruiting firms, she'd think I wasted her time. It hurts the relationship.

James Altucher says, "Let them both preview/agree to connecting." He calls it permission networking.

What I do with Cadre is curate who's in it. I attract people and identify if they have a pay-it-forward approach. Then everybody at the event can let his or her guard down.

People who want into Cadre are often referred in by an existing member.

I might say, "It looks like you have an interesting business and know some other Cadre members. Read our webpage and if it resonates, we'll schedule a phone call with you." And our webpage is mostly about who doesn't fit — including the price, because you don't want to invest time in people and then find out they can't pay $500 a month for membership.

My cowbell is giving without expectations. It's purely about helping other people. When I make intros, I love hearing it was a good fit and mutually beneficial. It's a rush and it feels good. If I've been in a rut and I go back and look at my network and connect people for 30 minutes on Facebook, I feel great. When I see a Facebook post where someone is asking, "Does anybody know a good person that does x?" I actually feel bad if I don't have time to find one for them.

I think most people, if they connected two people successfully, would get that same rush — but maybe a lot of people just haven't done it.

Leading up to book launch I was very self-absorbed, and a lack of me being a connector was manifesting. I've always been a big giver, so I earned the right to ask. It's not something I've done a lot. I asked my network to buy my book for others as a gift, and the readers sent feedback to those buyers that it was great for them. So, they're a hero for giving my book away. I always try to bake in a benefit for everybody.

## MIKE CARNEY – HELPING PEOPLE AND COMPANIES SUCCEED

Mike has been focused on providing online engagement Solutions since 1997. He's always had an entrepreneurial spirit but he put words into action in 2012 by launching his own company and now leads a successful performance marketing focused recruitment company called PerformanceMarketingJOBS. His passions are: Helping people, having a fun but stable family life with his wife and two kids, coaching kids' baseball and hockey teams, cheering on the Toronto Maple Leafs and Glasgow

Celtic and playing in the Celtic hoops any chance he gets. Here's his story…

My cowbell is that I love to help people succeed within the performance marketing industry. How I help them is by being a confidential recruitment partner between companies and candidates. Within a tight community the rumor mill is strong, so it's best to use a third party to source out candidates and to discuss career advancement opportunities through. Having lots of people know that you've applied somewhere is a great way to lose your current job.

My company is called PerformanceMarketingJOBS and it's a business that is hyper focused on the talent needs of the performance marketing space. Cost-per-hire recruitment services for cost-per-acquisition marketing companies, a perfect fit. For candidates, there is no charge and they can use PerformanceMarketingJOBS to have confidential conversations about their career advancement goals and to have their resumes submitted directly to decision makers – no more resume pile! For employers, in true performance fashion they only pay me when I deliver a hire.

Discovering the business was easy - making it a business was an extreme challenge. Having worked as recruitment consultant for quite a few years and by having employers ask me if I had candidate connections that I would recommend, it was easy to see that there was a great need for a full-time recruitment resource within the performance marketing industry. The huge problem was that there was very little history of entrepreneurial focused companies willing to pay for such a service. Typical affiliate and performance marketing companies' owners would normally wear 42 hats and recruitment was just one of them. Recruitment was a time eating task but not something that they were willing to pay someone else to do. Why the business eventually took off was because I was helping companies recruit for positions that I've actually done myself and because I was delivering solid results. Once businesses saw results and noticed how much more free time they had to focus on day-to-day business activities for minor things like – driving revenue – then word spread and the business took off.

I'm not a huge fan of the word failed so I'll use the word stalled. Failure to me is just being successful at figuring out what doesn't make money. Test, track, tweak.

For quite some time the business stalled - stalled as not making much money…For nearly a year. As an entrepreneur you find out quickly that knowing a business is financially viable and proving it are two completely different things. At times I just wanted to scale back, shift focus or just move on to something else as the business wasn't paying the bills and you can't buy your kids new clothes with love. Unfortunately retail stores cancelled that program a while ago. What I figured out over time was who my best clients were and then I focused on doing a great job for each of those clients. With results comes confidence, revenue, word of mouth marketing then more clients and more candidates.

I have two sets of clients – companies and candidates – and I treat them with equal attention and respect each of their unique needs. Now that most people in my industry know PerformanceMarketingJOBS as the go to resource for recruitment assistance it's a lot easier to gain new clients and get additional recruitment assignments from existing clients. In regards to candidates, where there was a drip of candidates contacting us, now there's a steady stream.

PerformanceMarketingJOBS is now a proven partner, the kids have new clothes, the future is bright and it's time to expand the business. I was originally hired to be a recruitment minion, now I need minions!

## How To Put Chapter Six Into Action And Get The Results You Want

- Think about your cowbell. What additional things does your cowbell require to succeed?

- Which of those are you really bad at, or hate to do? Who else do you need on your team? What is the specific talent you need them to possess?

- Do the people on your current team have the relationship they need to have with you? Are they getting help from you?

- Are you using your value to your teammates as an excuse to be a pain? "They have to deal with it because they need me."

- Is it possible the person on your team with difficult behavior is being fueled by your behavior? What can you do differently to improve the relationship?

- Are you clear with your team about what you need and how you need it?

- Are you clear with each of your teammates about what they need and how they need it?

- What are the strengths and weaknesses of each team member? Are there any weaknesses that no other team member is making up for?

- Is your team giving the customer everything they need?

- Is there an area of difficulty with customer service that might require adding another team member?

**Hey You, Did You Get Your Free Cowbell Principle Bonuses?**
As the owner of this book (even if you somehow got it for free) you are entitled to some awesome bonuses!

**#1.** The controversial chapter they made us take out! "True Secrets of Success That Make People Uncomfortable" You may not want to read this one... it's very unconventional. But it's all so true that it's funny. And if you're the kind of person that just wishes people would level with you, you'll love it!

**#2.** The Superfun Cowbell Overview Webinar

**#3.** Mystery BONUS! Better than mystery meat, guaranteed.

To get your free bonuses, go to thecowbellprinciple.com/bonuses and opt the heck in!

# 7. How to Make Sure Your Actions Create Your Own Happiness

This is a relatively short chapter, because we believe that happiness is a by-product of doing everything else the book suggests — which is all to help you find, develop, and flourish in your cowbell.

Look at Gene Frenkle, the cowbell player in the original SNL sketch. It appears that when you find your cowbell, you're going to have a pretty good time playing it! Why is that? Because you love it, you're good at it, and other people love it too. It's satisfying on every level.

The amazing thing about the book The Cowbell Principle is that it's already changing people's lives. We found a guy at a gas station who had been drinking. We explained the Cowbell Principle to him and he got sober and got his dream job in an hour! Normally when he does his cowbell, he gets arrested. But we suggested he do it this time while fully clothed.

Okay, that last story was not true. But the point is that you may have a cowbell you don't think much of because you have only exposed it to the wrong people.

Okay, that last paragraph is proof that having a good point does not always prevent your made-up story from going downhill. We're going to quit on this section while we're ahead.

### How Cowbells Increase Joy

Life is short and you live the life you create. So what better life can you create than one that's based on you doing something you love — that other people love too?

"Success is not the key to happiness. Happiness is the key to success. If you love what you are doing, you will be successful." — Albert Schweitzer

Didn't Gene Frenkle look happy playing his cowbell?

What a fool! Doesn't he know how stupid he looks? Maybe he does. Maybe it doesn't matter. Some of the most talented people and groups on earth look really stupid when they are at their best.

Any offense run by star quarterback Peyton Manning seems to be learning how to run the play for the first time right before the ball's snapped. It's one thing to call an audible and quite another to actually grab players and physically drag them into position. But it makes the fans happy and is valuable because it works.

The whole happiness-from-your-cowbell formula doesn't work if you have serious obstacles like true depression. And there are real circumstances in which it would be selfish and irresponsible to make drastic changes chasing after a cowbell. For many reasons, cowbell progress can be slow, but that makes it all the sweeter when you attain it.

For example, there was a time when Brian wanted to be a full-time freelance consultant but didn't yet have the network or assets in place to get enough gigs to do so. It was the responsible thing for him as a husband to take several full-time jobs and develop his career before going freelance again, this time successfully.

Over time, you can negotiate your obstacles and fulfill your responsibilities, moving toward the cowbell experience in a way that doesn't hurt anyone or leave any wreckage behind.

Until you are really experiencing joy in your own uniqueness, you won't shine, and you might not fully "get" how awesome a cowbellian life is. You need some self-esteem, which is best when it comes from action, but sometimes you have to start with ideas.

There's a type of depression that might not fit a clinical psychotherapist's definition. You might just be vaguely frustrated and feel low. You might be bummed out your life isn't more amazing. You might feel like you wish things would go faster. Affirmations and meditation and relaxing or inspiring music can help. As your life changes, as you take more action and feel better about yourself and your life, as your identity and self-esteem solidify, you can let go of those things. Deep inside you finally know that you are valuable and important. You no longer need Stuart Smalley affirmations.

## ANDY LIVENGOOD — OVERCOMING THE OPPOSITION WITHIN OURSELVES

Andy Livengood is an improv teacher and performer with Theatre 99 in Charleston, S.C. Here's hisstory…

People come to me to teach them, if they want to be funny, or get over their fear of public speaking, or get better at conversations, or break out of their shell. In some part, they come to me because I was chosen by Greg Tavares and Brandy Sullivan, the theater's cofounders, to be in the troupe or on more advanced teams or to be a teacher. They also come to see me perform too, for entertainment and laughs. You don't know where people are in life; often they're having a horrible time and just need to laugh.

I've been told people like to do improv with me because I'm a big support player. It's not common for improvisers but I will drop my idea to work on your idea. I love taking an opening line and thinking, "How can I add to this?" I can certainly initiate but I like to support. I ask myself, "What does this scene need?" Sometimes it needs me not to be involved. Sometimes the boss needs to walk in or the scene needs to end.

Audiences don't provide a lot of specific feedback after shows, but they respond to big and bold choices onstage. "That was funny when you…" Beginning improvisers aren't as willing to make a really bold choice outside their comfort zone and then have to live with it. I say just lean into it; do something just outside your comfort zone.

Why do I do improv? An amazing show changed my life. I went to see a show with a group called Moral Fixation that included Lee Lewis and Greg Tavares. They took improv from something that was funny to art; with just one line of dialog after about ten scenes, they revealed they'd been the same characters in every one of those scenes! There was suddenly a story arc and it blew my mind.

I like this quote from Teller, the quiet one in Penn and Teller: "Art is whatever you do after the bills are paid." I love to do improv. It's not my primary income now; it would be great if it were, but I'd do it for free.

And although it's not my primary income, it's more than just supplemental. The money I've made from teaching and performing and working at theater, including my one-man show, bought me my car. I have a day job 40 hours but all the improv money went to paying off a five-year car loan in 18 months… and my desktop and laptop computers. I crawled out of credit card debt because of the theater. I was making minimum payments, but the theater allowed me to knock out my debt in two years.

Before improv I was really self-conscious. I'd slouch into the corner. I had low self-worth. The idea that I might be funny or people might like me never would have occurred to me. This is probably true for a lot of people:

You're not as horrible as you think you are!

It's easy, when you have success, to get arrogant. I had a group, and we were king of the mountain. We felt we were breaking the boundaries of what is possible with improv. Initially with improv, I was terrified. Then I became more proficient. Then you say, "Oh, I'm good at this," which is healthy to say; then, next you get cocky. When everybody's hitting good, they all think they're amazing, but no one wants to play with a cocky performer. We'll choose someone good who's not a jerk over the jerk. We were young in our early 20s. And young people with talent can be real jerks.

I learned social skills. All you have to do to own the room is be positive, make eye contact, and don't mumble. Be a funny, friendly dude. Don't be overbearing; those people aren't confident, and they're overbearing to make up for it. I got to where I felt like I belonged. Confidence is "I'm fine; I belong here." All you have to do is listen, and give and take, and make eye contact.

Really, every significant friendship and relationship of mine comes from improv. You wouldn't recognize me if you knew me before. I was funny if you knew me — but you'd never get to know me because I was shy and self-conscious. I'd never be on the radar in a room. I was uncomfortable in myself. I had no confidence. I couldn't talk to a woman. I was overweight.

Improv changed my confidence, the way I stand when I enter a room; it taught me how to converse and how to listen, and I ended up getting into shape.

Now I'm comfortable in social situations. When you're making up scenes in front of 200 people, a regular conversation doesn't seem so threatening anymore!

In teaching, you have to be somewhat sure of yourself and proficient to teach. And teaching makes you better at it. I was a good improviser before teaching; now I'm better. You have to be analytical with what you do, back up your stuff when asked questions. Here's why I did this. It forces you to be better at it. Improv teachers teach what they're working on.

We should respect those who teach us what we really need to learn. However, the lesson is ours and our goal is to go beyond what is taught and not be limited by the imagination, knowledge, and experiences of our teachers.

## ALYSON LEX — ORGANIZE AND MONETIZE

Alyson Lex got her start working for two of the highest-paid and most sought-after copywriters and strategists in the biz, Dan Kennedy and Bill Glazer. As the marketing manager for their company, Glazer-Kennedy Insider's Circle, Alyson got a first-class education in all things direct response, and she's used that education to build her own business providing copywriting and marketing strategy to clients all over the world. She's been working on her education over the past five years, learning about online marketing, social media, relationships, and networking — you name it! She uses her techniques to help clients from Baltimore, Md. (her hometown!), to Australia make their marketing fun, effective, and profitable. Here's her story...

I've always been a problem solver. It's second nature to me; I see the big picture and the details and can present a simplified set of options as a solution. I play devil's advocate and look at the pros and the cons and find the holes from multiple angles.

That would make my cowbell the ability to organize, clarify, and monetize marketing and content. I make it profitable for people to be in the info business. I create a plan with a defined first step to get moving. Most people have an issue with just getting started, and I can help them get past that hurdle.

When I was younger, I was able to do something similar with schoolwork. In my writing class, I edited a friend's piece and gave it a different last line... for which she won an award. My line! I felt left out, so I stopped giving away my knowledge if I wasn't going to get recognized for it. (Because who doesn't want to feel like the smartest person in the world when you solve a problem?)

When I first entered the corporate world, these skills made me a great employee. I was consistently making my company better with new processes, new systems, and other ideas. At Glazer-Kennedy Insider's Circle, I created product out of content. It turns out I am cool with sharing my ideas as long as I get paid for it. It would be nice if the world thought I was super smart but that doesn't pay the mortgage. So they're basically giving me money for being super smart.

With my cowbell, I help a couple groups of people with related needs. One group has ideas but can't implement them. Someone may have a business but not want to be in it forever. For example, a chiropractor who is busy healing and teaching patients all the time might be ready for some financial freedom as well as more free time. I can take that practitioner's knowledge and create a home-study product for him to sell to his patients. I also help people with huge goals who are spread too thin and can't get it all done. Another group consists of people who can't think of what to do, like service providers who don't know what they could sell. Whether you realize it or not, there is an info product inside of you and I will drag it out of you and make you money.

I also help service providers like web designers. For example, maybe you're really good at conversions so of course your products should be about how to do that, but maybe you can't see that by yourself. Often, people who are proficient at something might not be able to see how they could productize it or teach it to people. That's where I come in.

## How To Put Chapter Seven Into Action And Get The Results You Want

- How many things do you have to do that you hate? Is there any way to offload them?

- Are you getting to do your cowbell enough, or are other things getting in the way?

- Are you worried because there are important things you're ignoring? Action is the leading cure for worry.

- Take a few minutes and write about your ideal day or week. If your life and work could be any way you wanted it, what would that look like? From the time you get up, through work, through family, friends, etc.

- What needs to happen for you to get to that ideal day or week?

## Hey You, Did You Get Your Free Cowbell Principle Bonuses?
As the owner of this book (even if you somehow got it for free) you are entitled to some awesome bonuses!

**#1.** The controversial chapter they made us take out! "True Secrets of Success That Make People Uncomfortable" You may not want to read this one... it's very unconventional. But it's all so true that it's funny. And if you're the kind of person that just wishes people would level with you, you'll love it!

**#2.** The Superfun Cowbell Overview Webinar

**#3.** Mystery BONUS! Better than mystery meat, guaranteed.

To get your free bonuses, go to thecowbellprinciple.com/bonuses and opt the heck in!

# 8. The Fine Line Between Creativity And Stupidity

Sometimes you need to get creative and intuitive and "really explore the space." In the "More Cowbell" sketch, that's what Bruce Dickinson implores Gene to do.

Ridiculous, right? Because the cowbell is a pretty limited instrument and probably needs to be close to a mic in order to get recorded.

We think what Bruce is really calling for is creativity: Some people may think that exploring the space means filling the room with your creative presence. Those people are mostly from Southern California. However, it does get you thinking about going beyond your perceived limitations.

Get out of your head and go intuitive!

## Creativity

Let's define creativity first, because believe it or not, this is a pretty controversial area.

Our favorite definition of creativity comes from Hungarian psychology professor Mihaly Csikszentmihalyi, the same guy who invented the concept of flow experiences (i.e., you're so euphorically into doing something that time perception changes). As he defines it, creativity is the combination of at least two old things in a new way. We would add that sometimes the method of combination isn't new, but the things you're combining are. For example, Mihaly's last name consists of letters in the standard English alphabet, yet no one has ever thought of putting them together quite like that before (or since). Additionally, his first name is pretty much half of his last name, making his surname the embodiment of his definition of creativity and, we suspect, causing everyone from elementary school teachers to airport security personnel to question their eyesight.

Some people hear "creativity" and think it only applies to someone like Van Gogh or Picasso — that somehow, painting is creative but designing the new Honda Accord isn't. For our purposes, we don't really want to argue about how creative something is. But we can distinguish between the applications of creativity, separating pure creativity from practical creativity.

Pure creativity — art for the sake of the enjoyment of art, like painting or classical music, often valued for the emotional experience only.

Practical creativity — an innovative solution to real-world problems.

Pure creativity may have a greater artistic value than a new Honda, but innovations in the design of your Accord may have a more practical everyday value to more people than Picasso has ever had. Even better, an old Honda won't cost $130 million.

Our first chapter on Demand made it clear that your success depends on providing something people really want or need. Our emphasis here is on practical creativity. You can be very innovative and have zero interest from the masses. For example, the lay-down commode got very little traction, and women never quite fell in love with open-toed cowboy boots.

Next question: Is everything creative something really new? How new does it have to be in order to be creative? Okay, so that's two questions. They're both important.

Initially, you might assume that creativity is about making something completely new, but it's not! When Van Gogh painted sunflowers, was that the first painting of a sunflower? Nope. But he painted it his way (a way that suggests some corrective lenses were in order). His work is highly respected, but it's still a matter of placing colored paint on a canvas, right? That's not new. It's only partly new.

The first time Garrison was served rat for lunch in Indonesia, he realized that there was no sauce on that table that could make you more comfortable with your rodent entrée. (Overseas cowbell opportunity, anyone?) Lunch is not new; eating something that lives in the sewer is — for most Americans, anyway.

Still, nothing is 100% new. People basically have always wanted the same things, such as security, sex, shelter, food, stories around the fire, and bacon. (We realize that's also a food, but some of us felt strongly that it deserved its own mention.) As society advances, we take our basic needs and answer them with progressively cooler, savvier solutions. We've switched from walking to riding horses to horse-drawn carts to automobiles to planes. Transportation isn't new. And cars aren't new. But the first time

Brian rode in a Tesla sports car, streaking down the streets of Finland at 80 mph in eerie silence — there was something new about this. And that's not the most practical example.

What about streaming Internet music? We've evolved stepwise from phonographs to tapes; from tapes to CDs; from CDs to iPods and mp3 players and iTunes. Now when you move, you don't have to box up 500 CDs. The floor of your car isn't littered with CDs, some of which are in the wrong cases. What the heck happened to my Beastie Boys CD? Shit.

Now mp3s and iTunes are fighting it out with streaming Internet music. A lot of people use Spotify or Rdio for this. Brian recently bought the new Coldplay album via iTunes but only because it wasn't available via Rdio. He pays Rdio about $15 a month to listen to anything and everything he wants, on his laptop or via his iPhone, as many hours a day as he wants. Very few artists, like AC/DC, the Beatles, and Led Zeppelin, are not available this way. We're pretty sure this is yet another innovation that hurts the major record labels' revenues; but on the flip side, it helps the smaller independent artists. Since streaming music began, the diversity of new music has increased, and the ability to discover similar artists with a click of the button increases the chances that any musical artist can begin to carve out a living doing what he or she loves.

Does creativity have to come from left field? Is it more creative to customize your Honda or invent a cat helmet for biking with your cat? Helmets already exist. Cats already exist. But the cat helmet is new. How new is it? How creative is it? Who cares! All we need to care about is how many people will buy cat helmets, and is your cowbell about creating animal headgear? A lot, and yes? Great! Another example of practical creativity is the invention of the vacuum cleaner. Businesses knew the housewife would be a major consumer, and carpet dust and dirt was one of the biggest household problems with the least efficient solution (carrying them outside and beating them — the carpets, not the housewives). The vacuum cleaner was so needed that it could easily be sold door to door.

Many successful startups are just slight twists on existing ideas, or an expansion of one website's small feature into an entire thing. AirBnB just got a $10 billion valuation, even though it wasn't a terribly original idea; craigslist had what they wanted to create, to a degree.

Is Picasso more creative than making ketchup bottles upside down so they pour quicker, or than the writers who worked on Breaking Bad? Let's just agree, to be constructive, that it's not important who or what is "more creative".

## To Be Creative, You Have to Put Yourself in a Creative Space

Go to the intuitive space in your mind. Do whatever it takes to get into that creative space.

Some people need to go to the beach house and pace barefooted on the floor to write their novel. By the way, how the heck did you get a beach house? Garrison is pacing and bouncing a Nerf ball as we write this. When your body is moving, your brain can move. Some people get their ideas in the shower.

Some can write sitting down. Others are weird, like Hemingway, who perched his typewriter on a chest of drawers and wrote standing up. While drinking liquor.

David Grohl of Foo Fighters and Nirvana did a great documentary called Sound City. It chronicled the history of Sound City Studios, a place where many rock-n-roll artists' best albums were recorded. This includes artists like Nirvana, Tom Petty, Neil Young, Red Hot Chili Peppers, and Paul McCartney. Strikingly, the studio was kind of a dump. But something about it inspired great creativity from some of the greatest artists in rock-n-roll.

Some people build music studios in their home because they feel more creative at home. They don't want the artificial feel of going into someone else's studio.

Some of the most creative rock music was written in the 1970s, possibly because people were on so many drugs, especially marijuana. Drugs altered how people thought, which in turn altered how they wrote. They also could be more creative on their albums; you only needed one hit per album. But rock-n-rollers were also trying really hard to get away from earlier music, and there was no formula for that yet. We now know certain chord progressions work, so hits can be written formulaically.

Still, even formulaic pop is creative. If you're the guy who writes pop songs for Britney Spears, you're helping tons of people who love Britney Spears. Maybe your cowbell is writing formulaic pop songs. But let's put aside snobbiness and admit that tons of people like music that other people think is crap. It's supply and demand. If it's your thing to create mainstream entertainment, go for it!

When Aerosmith's careers hit the rocks with drug addiction, sobriety, and then a completely ignored new album, they brought in a guy who said, "I love you guys. I know how to write an Aerosmith song." And the new writer brought about one of their biggest albums ever, Permanent Vacation. His cowbell was to love a band so much he could write new songs for them.

Similar things happened for Journey's current singer, Filipino Arnel Pineda, who was so good singing for a Journey cover band that when Neal

Schon saw him on YouTube, Journey contacted him and made him their new singer. And almost the exact same thing happened for Jon Davison, singer for a Yes tribute band who is the current lead singer for Yes, replacing original lead singer Jon Anderson. What are the odds that they'd both be Jons? Some people really do follow their passion and succeed incredibly as a result.

Butch Vig, the man and the drummer behind the rock band Garbage, also was a producer who helped indie and punk rockers into the mainstream, producing Nirvana's Nevermind, and bestselling albums for Smashing Pumpkins, Sonic Youth, and Jimmy Eat World. In 2012, music magazine NME placed him at No. 9 on its list of The Top 50 Producers Ever. His cowbell was about how he made things sound, which is an incredibly subjective thing. And that changed over time. But many agree that his approach to recording drum sounds, particularly on Nevermind, is one of the things that made the albums he's produced so popular. And notably, Garbage sounds very different from these other albums, so he wasn't a one-trick pony with his cowbell of sonic sensibilities.

### An Exploratory Mindset

To be truly innovative, you have to be in a creative mindset and have the willingness to look beyond what you've already done.

Are you willing to abandon what you've done before and what's been done in the past and to go in a new direction? If you do that, you can increase your success. It may be constructed of older parts. It's difficult to be creative if you're not willing to move away from what's been done.

Comedian Louis C.K. would develop an act, do it, then abandon it and do new stuff. It's dangerous; most comedians won't do it. In fact, your career could fail because of it, but his got better and better. He had a lot of stage time and enough life experience to make it succeed. Of course, his wife left him, too, and nothing makes comedians funnier than suffering. (The month George Carlin's mother died, he became a more powerful comedian.) Unlike Louis, most comedians would evolve their act, replacing weaker material with stronger material over time, rather than replacing the entire thing.

Richard Lewis was always trying new material, and audiences wanted their money back. Club owners want what they've seen on TV. Andrew Dice Clay's audience would mouth his entire act but still paid to see it. Seinfeld's audiences were laughing before the punchline because they already knew it. So he threw everything out.

It seems like many geniuses are most creative in their youth, before the age of 30. A lot of creative things happen in that time period. Is it that the brain is still growing? Is neuroplasticity (the ability to learn and change) yet to decline?

Drama or trauma may foster creativity in some. For example, if Garrison gets bad news an hour before a keynote and feels like he just should have died 10 years ago, he seems to be a lot funnier. The audience and the meeting planner are more overwhelmed by how funny he is. Why is this?

Richard Pryor grew up in a brothel, which they say is not good for kids, and he became a hilarious comedian. They say tragedy plus time equals comedy.

Your childhood doesn't have to look bad; the angst is sometimes internal. Some people are born with depression and other issues they fight internally, and they might never tell other people how bad it is. Their silent struggle might fuel their creativity.

While pursuing your cowbell requires both creativity and a willingness to move in a new direction, you want to ride an old idea as long as it's good, and then jump on the new one at the right time. If you've found something that works, work it — all the while developing something new that is not your main thing yet. (It might not even be public.) The intuitive part is knowing when to switch horses, when to make the new thing your main thing. Riding a horse is a skill and it takes practice, but eventually you'll have to switch horses. And maybe you get better at riding new horses.

If you've had a tough time in your life, or if you're having a tough time now and you don't have the positioning, influence, or circumstances you need, you are probably at your creative peak. So don't worry. You're going to be okay. You're in a perfect position to be creative.

If your life kind of sucks or has ever sucked, you have the building blocks for creativity. Congratulations.

Creativity is innate in all humans; we just have to have the willingness to unleash it. Like Bruce Dickinson said, explore the space! We all have the ability to do that.

## Rules for Brainstorming

Brian sometimes mentors first-time writers and coordinates corporate brainstorming sessions. These two areas have similar pitfalls and lessons. Here are 10 rules if you want to create a mind-blowing brainstorming session:

1.    No negativity. No analysis or criticism or comparing or editing of other people's ideas.

2.    All ideas are valid. We'll worry about what's good or bad later.

3.    Everyone contributes. Non-contributors should leave.

4.    No computers or tablets or cell phones. Phones off (not even buzzing). Have someone assigned to writing the ideas on a whiteboard. This person has no extra power in the brainstorming session and must contribute ideas too. Or, give everybody post-its and as they come up with ideas they can post their own post-its on a communal wall.

5.    Every idea is welcome, even dumb or crazy ones. Especially dumb and crazy ones!

6.    Build on other people's ideas. Combine ideas during the brainstorm.

7.    Come up with as many ideas as you can. Quantity not quality. It's a good idea to have individuals brainstorm by themselves before and after the group brainstorm.

8.    Take turns talking. Listen when not talking.

9.    Think future and forget the past.

10.    Resist tangents like storytelling and joking.

When you're writing or brainstorming, you must think every idea is good. You must separate the creating part of yourself from the criticizing part, or you'll get writer's block, and everybody in a brainstorming meeting is too afraid to vocalize ideas for fear of looking stupid. Everyone who's going to brainstorm has to agree to support everybody's ideas and vocalize all of theirs. Later you can judge those ideas. You're not making a commitment to the ideas yet— you're just sharing them.

Similarly, when you write, you should not be editing. Do these at separate times. Just get everything typed out. Fix problems and polish things up later.

A brainstorming session is not the time to try to look good. If there's someone in the room everyone's trying to impress or who they're afraid to anger or look bad in front of, even if (especially if) that's the boss, you need to get that person out of the room, or that person needs to affirm all the brainstorming rules we're talking about here. A quiet person of great authority in a brainstorming room is intimidating. If you aren't going to contribute ideas, don't go into the brainstorming room.

### The Cowbell and Innovation

The unwillingness to be creative is what stops innovation from happening. What does that creative unwillingness look like? Criticism, limitations, fear, and stubbornness. Here are some of the things people say when they're blocking their own creativity, or their team's creativity:

- "I'm concerned about how that will make us look."
- "I don't like any of these ideas."
- "That doesn't fit with our brand."
- "(Person in room) has a good handle on this" or "(Person in room), wow… your ideas are (any negative adjective, or positive adjective with sarcasm)."
- "I can't stand behind that."
- "I want to make it clear, that's not what I think."

It's perfectly fine to be concerned with your image and to stick to brand guidelines, but think about that after creating and before you make it live or publicize it. Create a safe space and time for creativity and innovation.

## From Zero to Innovation

How do you innovate, if you've never innovated?

1. What's the problem OR what's the thing you want to make possible?
2. What's missing from the current situation?
3. Brainstorm ideas.
4. What's the value of your innovation? Will your innovation step on the toes of those who could help or promote you?

That step 3 is the tough part, but it becomes easier if you are clear on steps 1 and 2. The purpose of step 4 is to identify who is going to care about your innovation, who will or won't use it, and how important it will be to them. The last step is about not stepping on your own hose — not shooting yourself in the foot.

## Innovation Borne Of Emergency And Boundaries

Innovation is more likely to happen when you have finite resources. You might be able to create more with more resources, but in reality most people who have too much are less motivated and their ideas are less groundbreaking. In World War II we needed anti-aircraft guns. We streamlined production in a day.

Running out of options will make you really creative.

As city after city fell to Napoleon Bonaparte, he would acquire the most useless soldiers because his army would absorb the militia of the just-conquered city. He put those useless soldiers in front for the next attack. The enemy would go at those guys and think they were winning, but then Napoleon would advance the two well-trained divisions he had positioned on the flanks. They would surround and capture the enemy, earning victory by way of a "collapsing line." That's a creative way to be destructive!

## What Gap Do You Need To Fill?

Be really aware of what doesn't exist. Step 1 is to identify what's missing. What can't be done? What can't be found? We need something we don't have. What's the gap? What innovation could fill it in?

If you don't know what people have or value, or what the market has, you may be creating something new to you, but it's not an innovation. For example, a lot of stand-up comedians have a Star Trek bit, but they're all very similar: "The actor you've never seen before who is now wearing the red shirt? He's going to die." At least 11 comedians used that joke. It's a funny observation they've all made; but after the first comedian uses it, it doesn't fill a gap.

## Is Your Innovative Idea Truly Useful?

The cowbell criterion of usefulness reaches back to the Demand chapter. You might have come up with a great idea but it had no application. The Puritans had buckles on their hats and buckles on their shoes, but they didn't wear belts. Now we buckle belts, not hats and shoes. We use them in a different and better way now. You could create something not applicable at the time. You could, like Nikola Tesla, seem more relevant a century later. That's innovation, sure — but isn't it better to create something that fills a need now?

There has to be a real need, a current need, for what you've come up with. It needs to be relevant when developed, not just in the future. Illustrating our point, we hope you use this book in 2014, not in 2814.

Innovating Is Not the Only Way to Make Money

Sometimes, it's not the inventor who creates the final usable product and profits from it; it's the implementers and financiers.

Orville and Wilbur Wright had a good idea, but Donald Wills Douglas made the fortune. Douglas is known for building Douglas Aircraft, which through mergers became McDonnell Douglas and, more recently, Boeing. The Wright Brothers' plane was light, like a big, motorized, gliding kite. Douglas created something stronger, faster, and more controllable.

Alexander Graham Bell and Elisha Gray both worked on telephone ideas and engaged in a race for the patent office. Gray received a patent for a water-based telephone (a significant time after Thomas Edison filed a patent for a mercury-based method), but Edison proved that the water-based method worked before Gray. Gray was not much of an implementer. Later Edison went on to use a different technology to create the telephone that went into mass production.

Some of the most successful entrepreneurs are not innovators; their cowbell is to recognize and invest in potential. J.P. Morgan didn't build his family's wealth — his father did — but J.P. loved new and different ideas. He financed much of Edison's work, and together they built General Electric. Through this and other ventures, Morgan expanded his family's fortune to the point that he could bail out an ailing nation: Morgan loaned the U.S. government $150 million ($3.8 billion in today's dollars) to stave off the stock market's Panic of 1906. Morgan didn't innovate; he financed and optimized Edison's and Gray's innovations.

## As You Explore the Space, You Might Invade the Space of Others

Bruce Dickinson advises Gene Frenkle to "really explore the space" — a line that's subtly brilliant when you consider the limited nature of a cowbell. It can be really loud or really soft. And there's just not much more to it. So what's the point being made? Loosen up and get artsy. See how it sounds in the whole space. Don't have boundaries with it. Gene lost his boundaries and started running into people. He filled the space, explored it, and invaded other people's personal space.

When you start to explore the space with something that has great limitations, you're liable to invade the space of others. With digital marketing, for example, we online marketers learned so much that we've invaded PR's space. We've stepped on their toes with our approach to social marketing. But we believe it's superior in its trackability, effectiveness, and affordability.

Your innovation might make something else look ridiculous or stupid. "No offense, but what I'm doing makes what you do look stupid. Don't take that personally." If you've been watching PR over the last 10 years, there's been a drastic change. Tons of PR specialists have transformed into social media specialists. Many of them proudly claim to no longer do press releases. Innovation demands that you adapt or die.

Think about a guy in a horse and buggy, feeling pretty capable, and then a 1912 Stutz Bearcat shoots past him doing 45 mph. Now he needs to adapt.

Your cowbell could be innovation or you could have a unique kind of innovation. How do you uniquely innovate?

## Anyone Can Innovate

With live groups, Garrison sometimes presents his "Innovation Exercise." He holds up a water bottle and says, "This is a water bottle. Imagine it's something else." Holding it up to his ear, he says, "Look, it's a phone." Holding it by his tie knot, he says, "Now it's a bow tie." Holding it on the top of his head, he says, "Now it's a bow in my hair."

Then Garrison instructs the group, "Find an object and imagine it's something it's not. Your pen is a cigar. Your coffee cup is a hat."

Once they've done that, he says, "Now that you know you're creative, think of something you could do differently in your business. What haven't you done yet? Leaders, what leadership tactic haven't you done? I don't care what it is — just make it be different." They do that and share some of their ideas.

Garrison continues, "One day you'll think you're all out of ideas. I want you to remember then that you're wrong. The human race is always coming up with ideas. If you get stuck, you have to take an action or you won't get out of it. Treading water is just a polite term for controlled drowning. You have to swim to survive. If you're not going anywhere, you're going to drown.

"We call it treading water because it's more palatable. We call it quiche because no one wants to buy egg pie. We call it life insurance because you can't call it death insurance. We wouldn't buy makeup if it was called ugly face cover. So look honestly at your situation and what you're doing or not doing and take action."

Using that exercise as an example, people who struggle to feel inspired innovatively can first examine whether their problem is truly a lack of inspiration or just pure and simple inaction. Either way, by then stretching your mind with a simple prop, you might discover your ability to explore a market space with a degree of genius you didn't suspect you had.

## A Genius Form Of Copycatting
Geniuses often do a type of copying that not everyone else thinks of. They copy the process. Anybody can copy the "what" of something ... and we call that theft of intellectual property. Geniuses copy the "how," unless it's patented. Don't copy WHAT a good idea is; copy the HOW that made it and make your own WHAT.

Why does creativity win? Creativity creates a competitive advantage. You find newer, faster, more impactful ways to do something. If you can protect it with a trademark or patent, you protect your competitive advantage.

What does creativity have to do with success? Yesterday's solutions created today's problems. Today's solutions create tomorrow's problems. It never ends, and you can't give up if you want to stay on top. Do people retire, or do they just get tired of solving problems and give up? "Oh shoot, another problem? Now I'm depressed. Well, I guess I'll let the young people deal with it."

## MARTIN SHERVINGTON — NETWORKING AND IDEATION

Martin Shervington, Law and Business Degree (Joint Hons), PG Dip Organisational Psychology, Master Practitioner NLP, has spent 15 years in this field working as an executive coach and marketing psychologist; he is now based between the UK and the U.S., dependent upon clients. He runs two communities: Plus Your Life and Plus Your Business, both on Google+. He trains, coaches, speaks, interviews and consults, and supports the communities on a daily basis. He also writes comedy with a psychological twist and performs a little stand-up when he gets the chance. Here's his story...

As a kid, at school, I remember being told my talents were best spent in the direction of the sciences, and definitely not the arts. So, from about age 13, I believed I wasn't creative.

I processed information, analyzed, and generally followed the steps I was given for quite some time. Then, in my 20s, like a jolt from a very rigid, turgid, and inevitable fate, I found that I had a lot of ideas. A lot of ideas I also put into action.

Ideas into action is something that has to be one of the most enjoyable expressions of being human. We come up with stuff, whether it is a business concept, a hilarious grumpy meme, or a joke, and we show and tell it to people around us — bouncing it around, giving it life and expression. This has been my creative expression for the past 20 years or so. Seth Godin talks of tribes and hives; well, over the past couple of years, the community on Google+ has enabled me to play with every idea, all the weird and wacky ones, and find out if people want to play along. If anything was my cowbell it would be the way I find people to play. I don't think it is unique or exclusive (i.e. you can do the same thing, too); I just feel honoured (yes, with a 'u') that I have people around me who trust me enough to try out new things on Google+, pushing our understanding of the social dynamic and how it relates to Google Search.

Businesses approach me and the team as we are keeping it fresh, bringing people together, and getting results in the new socialized web.

## SHIRA ABEL – A LOVE FOR GROWTH AND RESULTS

Shira Abel is the Vice President of Marketing at Musketeer - http://www.getmusketeer.com and the CEO of Hunter & Bard, a full-service strategy, marketing, design and development agency. She has been working in the tech start-up industry for over 15 years. Clients include: Musketeer, Nifty, oBTW, CloudEndure, Flayvr, two of the top 5 insurance companies in the world, and more. Shira is a thought leader and a sought-after speaker in the start-up marketing space and is regularly invited to judge at start-up conferences. She also mentored at Google Campus, the Microsoft Ventures Accelerator, and several other accelerators. MBA from Kellogg School of Management. Here's her story…

I started with mentoring. I already knew people from the industry by going to a million events and networking, and I wanted to give back. I didn't expect work from it. From the networking came speaking. Now all of my work and speaking gigs I get through referral. I don't go after companies, companies come after me. People choose to work with me because they trust me. They trust me because they've seen me speak, or have heard about me from people they know.

My cowbell is the combination of five things that together lead to trust and clients:

1. LEARNING: I love learning. I read and study obsessively. That's critical to being a thought leader. I'm constantly reading. I've been told by a few people that they like to follow my LinkedIn because I share what I'm reading. I have a strong belief in the growth mindset. I can learn anything.

2. SPEAKING: I'm opinionated and open. I give my knowledge freely. And I have no filter, which means I make mistakes on stage and ends up making me more tweetable. Maybe that would hurt me in an enterprise (that's up for debate) but the honesty and openness bring me higher trust value with clients. It's also part of what makes me entertaining.

I also grew up around very entertaining people. My brothers are both characters - one was an actor that now teaches drama and the other is "the guy at the party who tells stories and everybody wants to talk to." I learned how to improvise in college, where I took a course, and I've been using it ever since. I don't have a script when I talk, so I have no idea what I'm going to say ahead of time.

I love teaching in my lectures, and try to engage the conference even when it's thousands of people – because that just makes it more interesting for everyone. My lectures are thick with information – it's like a master class in marketing, starting with the fundamentals. I give the background information because I often work with hardcore engineers. Engineers and marketing often have a disconnect, and explaining what we do and why we do it (plus how to measure it) helps everyone get along that much better. Hence, I explain a lot.

3. DIVERSE EXPERIENCE AND EXPERTISE: I have a very diverse background. Including account management, customer service, sales, digital marketing and behavioral marketing (building marketing into the product, get people's behaviors to be what you need them to be).

I've been in tech for 16 years, and have experience working in and with a multitude of companies. I've brought significant growth in every company I've worked in. This is what has helped my reputation to get me to where I am now. I've traveled a lot so I understand different cultures and can see from their perspective. I've seen a lot of business models, how their marketing has been implemented and can help companies sort where they'll stumble, and how to mitigate that risk.

Right now I work on a company that is business to consumer, business to business and business to government. Not many marketers would be willing do all three. Having diverse background and skills make you more valuable. You can solve more problems than one person usually does. Years ago I left a job and found that they needed to hire three people to replace me.

4. RESULTS-ORIENTED. I'm more results-oriented than money-motivated. I'm cheap with other people's pocketbooks because I want them to make it, so if I don't think they need my skillset now I'll tell them to wait. And if they don't have the budget I'll give them alternatives. I have enough leads and work – I don't need to rip anyone off. I want companies to succeed and people to have jobs. I hate it when companies waste money. Put it aside for the rough times, which most businesses go through at one point.

As I mentioned, I'm obsessed with bringing results to companies. I've worked in a company where we lowered fraud by 40%, raised retention by 20% by changing our methods and implementing certain procedures. For another company we raised conversions by 20-30% by optimizing the website. I love working on optimizing the funnel. We've brought apps to critical mass of users by optimizing their inbound channels. I framework procedures they can implement.

5. PASSION: I love what I do. My very first job in tech, I was the Marketing Manager for a startup that needed to finish a product. We had 2 weeks to finish what should have been a 2 month project and it had barely been started. I slept on floor of the office for 2 weeks (there was a shower in the office, fortunately). That helped make my name in Israel. When things need to get done I will find a way to make it so. I have passion for my work, and people want to work with someone like that.

## How To Put Chapter Eight Into Action And Get The Results You Want

- Do you think of yourself as a creative person? If not, are you open to finding out that everyone including you is creative?

- Make a list of the products, services and processes in your niche. What would be a weird new way to implement each one? If you get stuck, think about how people do things in other industries. Is there anything you can borrow from there to modify something in your niche?

- List some innovations you can think of in any industry or niche. Write down what was new and different about each one. Can you do something similar with one of your products or services?

- Do something relaxing or fun. Then ask yourself, what's the craziest thing you could do to one of your products or services?

- Brainstorm 5 new product or service ideas.

- Brainstorm the 5 craziest things you could do with your cowbell. Write down things you think would never work, or you'd never have the guts to do. In those five crazy things may be the best idea you've ever had.

- Think about your cowbell. What's missing for you currently? Now ask yourself: How would Steve Jobs fix that? How would Thomas Edison or Nikola Tesla fix it? How would Einstein fix it?

- List the 5 most innovative companies or artists or musicians you can think of. What made them innovative? Could you copy their process?

# 9. More Cowbell: The Connection Between Excess And Success

You can never have too much cowbell, right? That's what Bruce Dickinson said.

Sure, you may have found your cowbell, but are you really paying the heck out of it?

Three things in the sketch create Gene's success:

- Gene's playing the heck out of that cowbell.
- Gene's in a band that needs a cowbell.
- Bruce, the person in charge, really wants that cowbell.

Are you positioned where your cowbell does enough for you?

You can play the heck out of your cowbell and be in a place where people don't want it. Or you could be in a place that needs cowbell and not have it.

Maybe some of Gene's coworkers think he's playing too much cowbell, but he's doing what the person with the money wants. When the person who knows what people will pay for says, "I gotta have more cowbell," you give him more cowbell.

Gene's not so worried about what others think. Whose opinion is important? Bruce Dickinson's opinion. And for you that means your mentor, your boss, and your market research.

## How to Have So Much Purpose That Not Even Death Can Stop You

Your cowbell may define your purpose in life.

After you're dead, people might still be reading what you wrote or remembering what you did and getting something out of it. Michael Jackson and John Lennon both had so much momentum in life that they've had new songs released years after dying.

And one of them performed live after he was dead. Michael Jackson's hologram performed at the 2014 Billboard Music Awards. We imagine attendee conversations went something like this...

"Didn't dead Michael Jackson do a fine job?"

"Yeah, for a dead guy, he was fantastic!"

That's saying something, because the average dead guy is so bad in front of an audience that people weep quietly and chat with each other. We're talking about a viewing. Okay, anyway...

You know you had a great cowbell if they're willing to put your hologram in a room and have people dance and clap to it. That's how a cowbell overcomes death.

## Why You Must Ask "Why?"

Why do you do what you do? It's important to have a reason for your career and life purpose. Know it. Believe in it.

If you don't know your "why," there's a pretty good chance your "how" and your "what" are wrong. You might not be doing the best version of your thing. You might not be going about it in the best way.

Suppose you're a really good dancer but you don't know why you love it so much. You just know you're meant to dance. But like many people, you're somewhat afraid of success. That's the real reason you're a dance teacher — because if you really dance because you love the feeling of freedom, you'll want to increase that freedom. You might not be able to do that as a teacher. You need to perform more. You might have to go out on a limb, compete, and maybe lose. You might need to take more risks. That's why you may do a different "how" and "what" because you really understand your "why."

You can be a great comedian, making money as a professional, but still not know why. Garrison was a great club comedian, but it hit him when he was on stage in Los Angeles at the Comedy Store, as the piano player in the Belly Room played "The Yellow Rose of Texas" for Garrison's theme music: "I remember I did pretty well and as I finished, it occurred to me — what is stand-up? If every 20 seconds you can get a house laugh [where the whole house laughs and the sound fills the room], then you're a star and they're going to bring you back over and over. But that's it. That's all there is to comedy. You're successful. There's nothing beyond that."

Garrison considered switching it up by making a point or being political within his stand-up material. But that's often the kiss of death. It hurt Bill Maher in comedy. He was funny, but his political stuff hurt him until he got out of stand-up and was primarily about political opinion for a while. Now he can introduce political material at comedy gigs because he has a following that agrees with him.

Garrison knew there was more to what he was supposed to do. "I was playing the hell out of a cowbell in an arena I couldn't have enough effect on. My how and what weren't as powerful as they could be," he recalls. So he explored why he was in stand-up.

He had stumbled into an open mic event and was pretty good at it; he was earning a living at comedy within a year, but he considered that part talent and part luck. He enjoyed being in front of an audience and liked the reactions he got, but he realized he felt out of sync with the bar scene. "I was in an environment where it was weird to be sober. I felt like I was dealing with sleaze balls and dishonest people," he said. "My booking agent would tell me to be sure to get into one lady's office before 5 p.m. or she won't write you a check. The same lady also hit on every comedian. It was a strange environment."

Once Garrison questioned why he was in stand-up, he did some corporate events, drawing on prior experience training salespeople in corporate America. It was better. He liked it. He was more successful. In fact, he made more money in an hour than he made in a month of doing stand-up.

Another aspect to the "why" of your cowbell is that you may actually be doing your cowbell when you realize you also have some specific purpose, a mission you want to pursue, but you haven't combined it with your cowbell. And when you do, you will do your cowbell differently to achieve that purpose.

Maybe you're the CFO of a corporation, but when you get down to it, what you really love is maximizing cash flow, and you're great at it, and you've saved your company's butt many times with this cowbell. When you think about all the things you've done in your job, this has only been about 5% of your work. Then you start thinking about what you might have to change to be doing your cowbell 60% or 80% of the time. You'd have to be a consultant, or switch companies more often. You begin to question your "what." And that's scary — but nothing great can be achieved without risk, which is one of the lessons of economics and the stock market that you as a financial person should already understand. We can't make you take the leap, but we can ask you to think about it.

## Releasing Your Power

Once you know what you're good at that's useful to other people, and you're getting paid for it, you can go as far and fast and hard as your passion will take you. It's amazing how hard you'll work when you're working for yourself, when you're the primary beneficiary.

You don't have to be an entrepreneur, but you do need to realize that when you work for other people, if you are a driven person, about 80% of what you produce is going to the owners and stockholders of the company. If you're more motivated in a situation where you make more money for doing more and doing it better, you should get into an environment that's more entrepreneurial and less corporate.

Here's something strange: Being a passionate cowbell player (in the metaphorical sense) who gets paid for it can look like being a workaholic: You might do it at all hours and think about it constantly, but you're doing it for the right reason.

And is it really addictive? We believe that addictive behavior and stress depend on your filter. They say stress is bad for you; is it? Some people jump out of airplanes and love it. Garrison would never jump out of an airplane that's working properly just to see if he didn't die. He went down the rapids once and loved it — but his wife was gray in the face and terrified.

Stress is not stressful; it's an interpretation, a filter. What's terrifying to some can be exhilarating and inspiring to others. If somebody is addicted to going to the gym and getting things done, that person is probably going to do pretty well with that. There's always the weirdo who shoots up steroids, but most gym "addicts" will just be healthier and feel better about themselves.

There are positive compulsions.

On the other hand, there are negative ones. You can be addicted to yogurt-covered almonds, or pizza, or screaming and yelling at people, or having sex with people you don't really want to have sex with. Certain addictive behaviors can stop you from ascending to a certain level, and others can help you get to a higher level. You can become president by being a workaholic ... but not by being an alcoholic.

## Monitoring Your Feedback

Here's an analogy Brian likes that's a bit obscure for some folks: negative vs. positive feedback loops. In other words, thermostat vs. the Jimi Hendrix guitar noise. The thermostat turns the heater off when it's hot enough. That's a negative feedback loop. It promotes homeostasis. Jimi

Hendrix's guitar noise, on the other hand, is positive feedback, because the noise is being amplified by the mic, which is being amplified back into the mic over and over and over. A positive feedback loop pushes it to its maximum level.

Suppose you're in a regular job and you try to do your passion at night or on the weekends, but it makes you tired and you do poorly at your job and your manager puts you on probation and you have to stop doing your passion. That's negative feedback. You're stuck because of that job. What you're doing keeps producing the same result. You're stagnant. But if you get fired with a severance and that gives you four months to create a new business, and it works out and you love it, now you can work on it all day and all night and get more and more benefit from that. That's positive feedback.

Habits can hold you back. Say you like to overthink things and make them so complicated that people don't know what you're talking about, so they leave while you're talking and consequently you have no influence. If you get clear with your speech and use everyday examples, people will like what you say and be more willing to pay for it. They can give positive feedback because they understand.

If the cowbell sketch had no Bruce Dickinson, the lead singer would diminish Gene's cowbell. He didn't like the aggressively loud cowbell. When you don't have the Bruce Dickinson, you end up with some dude with bad hair telling you what to do. Without the Bruce Dickinson, you are at the mercy of the influencers who don't have your best interests at heart. What you do really well, the biggest contribution you can make, is not on their agenda. Their deal is to make a profit using you as a tool. They don't care about your dreams.

You might have a really bad manager, in which case you need someone in your life who can encourage you. Never get into a situation where there's no Bruce Dickinson. Where is the Bruce Dickinson? You need an advocate for you who believes your cowbell is part of the key to success. Advocates encourage you and motivate you. They're in your corner; they believe in you and want to see you succeed.

## Mentors — The Good And The Bad (But Mostly The Good)

If you don't have good mentorship, you can still kind of cobble a mentor together from an assortment of people who have what you don't (or what you need more of). Garrison did this. Because he disagreed with people too much and did things his own way, he had no strong mentorship from a single entity. So when he realized he was missing some components of success, he found people who had the talents or resources he was missing to be successful. If you don't have a mentor leading you through, you need to identify what you're bad at and then arrange to get those things.

The main reason we don't have mentors is our aversion to mentorship — pride and ego and the fear of being misled. The more of an original thinker you are, the more out of the box you think, the more difficult it is to feel a mentor is on your side. Mentors try to guide you in a direction, but some percentage of people are just wacky; their thinking is a little off. If you find yourself being one of those people for whom mentorship isn't working, find a mentor anyway, because your original ideas won't be squelched like you think; you can take the guidance you want and leave the rest. Some guidance is always better than none at all.

It's always good to get feedback. Sometimes people are wrong when they try to advise us, because they're stuck in their own filter. The truth about things is not as prevalent as the belief system that person is using to feel better. Their faulty input can temporarily discourage you; but if the other person is wrong, you'll return to that right thing and continue on eventually.

## No Such Thing As Perfect Knowledge

Brian found that in using website analytics for 15 years to try to track what businesses do online, there was never perfect knowledge. There were always discrepancies and questions. There's a lot we don't know. We make decisions without all the facts. We have beliefs and best practices and theories.

You fall in love with someone based on who you think that person is. When you find out who he or she is, can you live with that? Is it good for both of you? If so, you can be married a long time. If not, it can be very expensive.

A drunk surgeon on a plane once told Garrison, "Half of surgery is exploratory. Those anatomical drawings are a lie! They're an approximation, at best. You open people up and they're different in there, so you have to change your plan." Equally perplexing is the fact that people have vastly different immune systems. One guy is allergic to shrimp and gluten, and another guy can eat out of a garbage can in an alley and never get sick. We're not the same. Because of this, knowledge is only half the battle. The other half is effort.

We have different compositions, capabilities, mindsets, intelligence levels. Effort is the great equalizer. We have the ability to apply what we do have, as much as we can apply it. Who's rich and successful? Effort. Why are some of the less athletically gifted athletes doing better than the #1 picks? They're willing and able to apply more. Good motor. Hustle.

Urban Dictionary defines hustlin as "havin [sic] the ambition and drive to do everything and anything to make mad money."

Gene Frenkle, a guy who'd eaten too many burritos and bought too small a shirt — he put the effort in. He played the hell out of the cowbell. Bruce Dickinson says we need more cowbell. Together they increased Gene's opportunity because Dickinson fueled Gene's enthusiasm, effort, and zest.

When a Bruce Dickinson spots enthusiasm, your opportunities increase. Every manager wants an employee who will work hard.

Garrison once won employee of the month, although other coworkers were more productive. Why was he singled out? He worked until 10 p.m. all the time and management noticed. It was really because he was bad at time management, and he just couldn't get the work done during the day. He wouldn't leave until he got it done. His effort and persistence got noticed.

Brian's favorite time to work is Friday night into Saturday and Sunday, because no one else seems to be working then, so no one interrupts him and he feels like he's getting ahead. Workaholism is bad if you're a bad husband or a bad parent, but Brian and his wife don't have kids and both love to work.

Would you rather be hopeful or successful? Would you rather have something good in your life now, or the possibility that something good might happen in the future? Do you prefer achievement or potential?

It's easy to unconsciously choose hope in ways that keep you from success. If you are content with hope, you might not finish something. You might go off and relax or entertain yourself instead of pushing through to success.

Those who succeed are impatient for achievement. They make it happen sooner. If you want to be more successful, you cannot be satisfied with hope or potential. You must push to get your results now. You must feel like you deserve more — now.

What this means is that when the "hope" type of person sees someone who's discontent or impatient or pushy, it could mean the latter person is a "success" type. Success types can be irritating, no question. But they are often leaders for this reason.

## Irrational Optimism

Confidence is contagious. So is depression. Some people's cowbells include incredible confidence and positivity. Even if it's not yours, you will do better in life and career if you believe in yourself. Do whatever it takes to make that happen.

Garrison knows a guy who went from the mail room to CEO by talking nice about people behind their backs. Try that out!

One of the most valuable takeaways from the world of finance is that the biggest risks create the biggest profits. To win big, you have to play big. Those who risk the most win the most.

Brian believes that confidence and hope is so important that you should do whatever you need to do in order to have it. Some people do religion or spirituality. Some people drink green tea. Some take antidepressants. It doesn't matter what it is. Without hope and confidence, everything you do will be at least 30% crappier. You won't do it with your full faculties. Your skill won't be accessible. People won't respond with excitement. Do whatever it takes to feel positive, then do your best work.

If you aren't familiar with the concept of flow, let's return to some ideas put forth by Mihaly Csikszentmihalyi. Mihaly is important to the Cowbell Principle in two ways. As discussed in an earlier chapter, he defined creativity really simply. And, more important to the current discussion, he defined flow, which is the fun and the dopamine release and the "time flies" perception that you experience when you're doing something you love and are good at. We don't have any proof, but we think it's good for your mental and physical well-being, and of course you get all the benefits of the cowbell principle itself.

The only thing you have to lose from being irrationally optimistic is you might be disappointed sometimes. But there is so much to gain, it's worth it!

The main reason Brian doesn't mind giving up weekends for work — prefers it, actually — is because he loves what he does. As Steve Jobs said, "It's more fun to be a pirate than to join the Navy."

## Today's Solutions Produce Tomorrow's Problems

"It is not the strongest of the species that survives, nor the most intelligent, but the one most responsive to change." — Charles Darwin

Let's return to an idea put forth in the Creativity chapter: The solutions of today are creating the problems of tomorrow. What you're doing right today will be wrong tomorrow. Human beings have more and more problems to look forward to, but also more solutions.

We've ascended pretty high on Maslow's pyramid, and now our big problems are things like, why the heck do all these cords keep getting tangled up? Forget the fact that this means we have a ton of electrical devices, and that means we're relatively rich and can do amazing things with common technology… we have high-quality problems. First World problems. Now we just need everything to be wireless without everyone getting brain cancer. That's the next problem to solve.

Sometimes success is a bigger problem than failure. Failure means you still have a familiar problem and you've eliminated one of the possible solutions. Success means you have a totally new situation to come to grips with and you have to start thinking of new ideas to solve your new problems.

Once you achieve a level of success that's new to you, you might be tempted to stagnate. You might not even realize you're stagnating. After a while, it might occur to you that you don't have a goal anymore. The key to continued success is to keep making bigger goals. Raise the stakes. Not only will it increase your success, but other people will help you more when they know what your goals and obstacles are.

The good news is that often the same reason you wanted to achieve a certain level of success is the same reason you'll want more. To get more, you have to raise your game. It never gets easier because you keep challenging yourself. Eventually you get used to that, but succeeding after your first big success is the hardest thing. Take it to the next level.

## The Skill Gap

Both Brian and Garrison have worked with PrideStaff, one of the top 25 recruiting firms in the United States. In helping PrideStaff achieve its goals of finding more candidates to send to employers, we learned that one of the biggest problems in the work world today is a lack of skilled candidates. Sure, tons of people can work at McDonald's or type on a computer, but companies need workers with specific education and skills. Many employers have unfilled positions because they simply can't find enough people with the right skills.

One problem is that not enough people are availing themselves of the opportunity for further education. You can find yourself a competitive advantage just by being willing to get more training.

There's also been a cultural shift. Many younger people now prize free time with their friends above career advancement. For them, free time is more valuable than work. They don't want to go to night school or take courses online. They'd rather find a company that trains them on the job. Employers are realizing they're going to have to hire for talent and train people on the job, but not all companies have made this shift yet.

The good news is that if you're willing to get more training, you'll have significantly greater opportunity. If there were ever a time to get more education, it's now, because the best place to compete in business is where the competition is weak.

When applying for a job, if you can say, "Right now, I'm taking an online course in (whatever you're applying for), and I'm halfway through," you'll be more likely to get the job. There's a ton of competition for jobs now, so give yourself that advantage.

## How to Set Boundaries and Charge More for Your Value

If only it were infrequent that we saw our peers in consulting complain that people are taking advantage of them and getting their advice for free. It's easy. Just stop doing it.

We understand — if you aren't busy, it makes you feel important to play your cowbell for them. But it also devalues you, in their eyes and in yours.

If you have a value, if you should be paid, then stand up for that. Say no to people "picking your brain." Sorry, brain surgery is expensive... and if you think there's something valuable in my brain, then pay for it!

The people who refuse to pay you weren't going to be your customers anyway. The ones who are offended are the ones who take advantage of people. It doesn't matter what those people think.

Or you may be asked for free help by a salaried employee who doesn't understand how entrepreneurs charge for what they do. Educate them.

If you set the right boundaries, you'll make more money — or at least you'll save time and have a chance to do the things that can help you make more money, like marketing or blogging or creating more services and products.

## DAVID MEERMAN SCOTT — ROCK STAR SPEAKING

People in the marketing and PR fields are well aware of David Meerman Scott and, in particular, his book The New Rules of Marketing and PR, which, now in its fourth edition, is one of the bestselling marketing books of the last 10 years. Here's his story...

I'm a marketing and sales strategist and I deliver my information in three ways:

1.     Via the Web for free, with a blog (www.webinknow.com), videos (vimeo.com/dmscott), and social networking such as Twitter (@dmscott);

2.     Via my books (nine of them so far); and

3.     Via my live speeches.

I realized that my cowbell was my ability to entertain with my content. For example, with speaking, I do not compare myself to other speakers. Rather, I compare myself with rock stars.

I'm a huge fan of live music. I've seen nearly 500 bands and am interested in how musicians and bands perform, as well as how they market themselves. So that's who I compare myself to. I've learned a great deal from people like Amanda Palmer and Mick Jagger and bands like the

Grateful Dead.

When I go to a live show, I watch how the musicians interact on stage and I adopt some of the moves in my own live speeches. For example, Mick Jagger knows exactly where he is at every moment. There is not a wasted gesture, move, or step. He knows where the other Stones are, where the spotlight is, and most of all what the audience is doing. He's probably the most self-aware performer we've ever witnessed. He's a complete pro. So many speakers resist rehearsal because they don't want to get stale. Jagger shows how counterproductive that attitude is.

Another example: I caught Tyson Ritter of the All-American Rejects at a recent Boston show (thanks to my friend Jodi who manages the band and invited me to watch from the photo pit). Ritter sometimes went way out front, standing on a monitor and interacting with the audience. I learned to do the same. Now I love to stand on a monitor and interact with the audience.

I've got no musical ability but have always loved watching how rock stars move and interact. How cool that I can do the same but in a different business! In the hundreds of events I've spoken at, I've never seen another speaker jump onto a monitor. I learned the move from someone outside my "competition."

Another example: I looked to the Grateful Dead for inspiration about sharing content. Learning from the Dead, I give lots of content away for free (with no email address required).

I'm convinced that by learning from musicians and bands, I've developed a more personal style than had I just copied other business authors and speakers.

I have paid speaking engagements nearly every week. And I get fantastic feedback from event organizers.

David's impact on meeting planners and audience members gives evidence of the effect of his cowbell. A few comments we picked from his site reflect how expertly he has worked his passion for live rock performances into his cowbell ability to entertain through content:

"His high-energy speaking style is engaging, entertaining and enriching. He left the audience spellbound... David's high-octane delivery grabbed the audience from the moment he stepped onto the stage, and didn't let go for 45 minutes... Forget about the 'guru' tag, David is a Social Media Marketing Rockstar! ...upbeat, exciting and motivational... The energy was awesome."

The combination of being informative and entertaining is a powerful one for a speaker. In fact, many speakers use it. But David's books and the influence of rock music on him help make him the unique speaker he is.

## JIM BOYKIN—TECHNOLOGY AND ADAPTING TO CHANGE

Jim Boykin started in the Internet Marketing and SEO Industry in 1999 when he formed We Build Pages. In 2011, the company re-branded to Internet Marketing Ninjas. Ninjas has grown to over 100 in house marketing ninjas with specialties in SEO, Link Building, Social Media Marketing, Content Creation, Digital Asset Creation and Marketing, Usability Analysis, Web Design, Community and Brand Building, and much more In 2012, Internet Marketing Ninjas also acquired some of the largest communities in the online marketing industry including webmasterworld.com, devshed.com and cre8asiteforums.com. Here's his story…

On a personal level, I love to teach and train people, and I love to dream of new things and make those new things happen. I thrive on constant change. I also have a unique gift for creating tools based on our own needs. We've built internal tools plus over 130 free tools we give away. We're the "good guys" but also "one of them" (the SEOs we work with).

On a business level, I consider us the "best" at content marketing. People come to us because they need to get citations (by way of things like links and social mentions) to help their branding and their rankings in search engines. We have a unique set of talent at our company that is more experienced than that of any other company in the world, including several "All-Stars." We have many employees who have been with us six or more years. We have proprietary and private internal tools that give us a competitive advantage. Our brand and our employees make us the most popular name in our industry — even more popular than competitors that are 50 times bigger than us. We also own several online communities, such as WebmasterWorld.com, SEO Chat, Dev Shed, Cre8asiteForums.com, and others. We own several of the world's largest communities in the online marketing and programming spaces.

Unique gifts people need and want from me are my training, strategies, insights, and ideas. I also excel at anticipating change, staying ahead of change, and bridging the gap between programmers and others.

As an agency owner, I'm able to keep talented thought leaders happy. I try to get the right people into the right seats on the bus, so to speak. If you have good people and it's not working, just move them to the right place, as Built to Last and Good to Great say.

For many years, I tried to hire only B-level or C-level level people, not A-level people. I was afraid of a smart person taking my knowledge and going out on their own. Then I heard Steve Jobs say, "If you don't hire A people, and every level below you hires a lower-quality person… it just degrades." Hiring B and C people won't grow your company. So I started hiring A people. And it turns out that sometimes, your biggest fear happens: You hire them, train them, and they do go out on their own. But we've grown. We used to be just a link-building company, and now, we're a full-service company: content, customer service, analytics, sales, and social media.

Looking at other companies, I know their work is handled by kids who don't have too many years of marketing experience. Our firm, Internet Marketing Ninjas, has world-renowned experts and works with amazing in-house SEO teams.

One of my cowbells is bridging the gap between programmers and others. Programmers speak a different language sometimes, but I can look at my teams and see what needs to be programmed: "Oh, we can automate this or add this feature to save you time and increase your work quality." One-third of our team is designers and programmers working on internal tools.

A little while back, I bought some communities like Dev Shed, and they were filled with ads that took away from the user experience. I removed the obtrusive ads and gave the users back their communities. That made Jim Boykin a cool guy with the programming and development community. If you stay true to the community, you get the karma.

When clients see our tools now, they say, "Wow, where do I get these?" Some are internal proprietary tools that give us a competitive advantage. But I decided a lot of them I could give away to the public. I had always held back, but in 2003, we started releasing free tools. That helped our marketing because people cited us and we got a lot of links from bloggers and resource pages, which helped our search rankings. We have 130 free tools online, and we're releasing our pro tools in January 2015.

## Growing From the Ground Up

I went to college for marketing. This was pre-Internet. I was the computer lab guy. I then traveled the country for four and half years goofing off, not knowing what I'd do for the rest of my life. I enjoyed traveling and working at national parks. I'd head west, then work, head north and work. At one point, I ended up living out of my truck in San Francisco and collecting food stamps because I was broke. In New York, I waited tables, because that's where the money was, in resorts.

I never thought I'd have 100 employees. I still walk around the office sometimes and I'm like, "How did this happen?" I happen to be in the position of being CEO of a 100-person company. It just grew over the years.

When I got a computer and got online in 1999, I was instantly like, "I found it... this is what I'm going to do for the rest of my life." And within a few months, I discovered the world of Internet marketing. I thought, "Wouldn't it be cool if I was doing website design and Internet marketing?" So I went to chamber events and the Center for Economic Growth trying to pick up business. I didn't stop working to be the best at this; I was addicted to learning everything I could within my industry. I was then able to go from waiting tables five days a week to four days a week, to three days a week, to where for a while, I was working one day a week just for fun and exercise and because I loved the people there.

In 2002, what was then called We Build Pages went from #240, to #80, to #22, to #2 on Google for the phrase "Internet marketing." I had to stop waiting tables, and I had to hire people. I went from trying to support myself to employing six people within six months and making a nice profit. My general manager today was my restaurant manager when I waited tables. I thought, "This guy, one day, it'd be so cool if he was working for me. He's a MANAGER. He's the perfect guy." I have a guy in customer service who was the bartender at a place I worked at. Our accountant was one of our waitresses at my old job: She could handle so many tables and was a workaholic, and she's multitasking-talented. I had found great people and great workers and managers years ago, and I later was able to utilize those people for our company. It took years to put some of the right people in the right positions, especially managers. But I have wonderful people who are so dedicated to me and the company. I think that's a huge key.

### Process of Evolution

Part of marketing the company is marketing myself. Almost every month, I'm at a conference speaking onstage. I have to give away great nuggets of information. At Affiliate Summit East 2014, I was the #1 session.

I used to stutter a ton when I was younger. To say a sentence would take minutes. After choosing computers, I never thought I'd have a job where I'd have to deal with the public. I look at the audience these days and can't believe I'm speaking to hundreds of people. But I feel like I have to be still thought of as a thought leader in the industry.

When Google's Panda update came out, I could see we were going to lose some clients. When people lose 90% of their traffic, they're going to run out of money. So I thought, "I need to become a specialist in this." I started writing, interviewing, and speaking about it. I became one of the leading experts on Panda.

When Penguin came out, that had to do with links. We were the link-building company. I'd built more links than anyone in the world. Now, we needed to come up with other methods. We saw it right away and figured out the response. Others had to learn their lesson. We had a head start on knowing what to do. I feel we're offering something that's Penguin-proof. And now, I've removed more links than anyone in the world.

Change happens. People complain, "It's harder. SEO is dead." Well, with every change, there's opportunity. Find it and capitalize on it. My specialty is Google updates. We're going to get more business as a result of them because we know more than anyone else.

I'm not afraid of Google updates anymore. My competitors are smaller because their clients are going through changes and they're not experts on the solutions. Competitors are laying off half their staffs, but we're capitalizing on change. You work harder. You don't get stale. You become the expert.

## Rolling With the Changes

I'm the entrepreneur, spirit, dreamer, idea guy. I walk in and say, "We're going to change the way this group works," and they go, "Oh no, Jim is making another change... but we know his changes work."

We experiment. Keeping our clients happy is a big thing. Then, we're profitable because they trust us and our recommendations. A lot of companies hand us a lot of money each month and say, "Do what you think is best." I lay out a roadmap and they say, "OK, we trust you." People who start small with us grow and increase their budgets. Our services change and evolve, and we don't get stuck in any one thing, and clients benefit from that.

This is the second-fastest-changing industry (nanotechnology is #1). It changes so much. The stuff that worked in 2008 can get you penalized today. Now, there's social media, new Google updates... there's constant change. What is the best thing to do today? What's going to be good for tomorrow as well? I love change, but change is hard for the average worker.

I'm always thinking how to offer better things, how to improve the tools. Our customer service team expanded. It used to be that we sold links and got you rank, and there wasn't a whole lot to talk about. Now, we have a whole client service team.

I'm rediscovering my cowbell all the time. I tend to be on a three-month schedule at work. For three months, I focus on certain groups, and then I move on to other groups or things with my time. I used to do all of the training until early 2009. I recently discovered that a lot of great knowledge has been lost over the years. I forgot how much I loved training: I took new hires in content marketing and trained them and enjoyed it so much. With them, I did the interviews and training, and I was excited about it: It had been six years since I'd done it. I suggested 50 articles and did five videos on a recent Saturday between 8 p.m. and 1 a.m. I'm excited to be on the front lines. And next month, I'll be in another area.

Often, when I'm talking to a client, they've already talked to sales and client services and analysts. When I'm on the phone with them, I do 80% of the talking, giving them tons of information: "Do this and that. Have you thought about X or Y? Here's a million things." I love it.

I never want to be seen as "that old guy" or, "He used to be an influencer, used to be a thought leader, but now, he's a CEO." I am a CEO first, but I'm still a damn good SEO. This is my life and passion. I don't have hobbies outside of SEO. I do it on my own sites. My friends are in this industry.

Internet marketing is never going to die. There will always be people trying to get found on the Internet. Things will change: Roll with the changes and adjust and there will always be a place in the business for you. Don't become outdated. Stay on the cutting edge of your industry. I never want people to say, "He's not on the cutting edge anymore." I want to deliver cool tips people haven't thought about or don't know about.

Recently, we made a big change to our content marketing. We had a bonus structure. We did a three-month test four years ago, and that bonus structure worked so well that we kept it. Now, it's been thrown off and wasn't paying out as much, so I changed it so that we were still giving out as much as a year ago. My people are making money with the new system. There's still resistance to it, though! It changed things. I say, "But I'm giving you more money!" People fear change, so you have to reassure them, "We believe in it. We believe it's going to be good. We're going ahead and doing this change. Hold on."

I tell people, if you don't like change, you may not like it at Internet Marketing Ninjas. Here's a new way to do this. Here's a new service. I may sell a service before we actually do it. Sales says, "But we don't have that." I say, "Well, we need to do it." Not all of my crazy ideas pan out, but enough work out to be profitable.

I come up with a lot of ideas. Because I'm the CEO, I can make those dreams come true.

## How To Put Chapter Nine Into Action And Get The Results You Want

- Do people want your cowbell where you are?

- Where do people want the cowbell you have? Can you go there?

- Why do you do your career?

- Why do you do your cowbell?

- Does your career fit your cowbell?

- Do you feel like you understand your purpose and are fulfilling it? If not, what's missing?

- Imagine doing your cowbell more and getting paid more for it. What else is in this mental picture? What things do you imagine you'd need in your life, and how can you get them?

- Are you benefitting enough from your cowbell, or is someone else cashing in on it more? Is there a way for you to get a higher percentage of that?

- Do you love your cowbell enough to do it through lean times? Does it motivate you to sometimes forget to eat or sleep because you love it so much? If not, it may not be a cowbell.

- Do you have a mentor that's helping to maximize your output?

- Are you motivated even when you aren't talking to your mentor? If not, you may not have enough inner drive. Find something you really love and create some challenging goals.

- Do you have problems now that are higher quality than a year ago? If not, you're not moving forward.

- What skills do you have that make you more valuable than other people? If you don't have any, you need to develop them!

- Do you say no most of the time when people want you to do your cowbell for free? If not, get some boundaries!

**Hey You, Did You Get Your Free Cowbell Principle Bonuses?**
As the owner of this book (even if you somehow got it for free) you are entitled to some awesome bonuses!

**#1.** The controversial chapter they made us take out! "True Secrets of Success That Make People Uncomfortable" You may not want to read this one... it's very unconventional. But it's all so true that it's funny. And if you're the kind of person that just wishes people would level with you, you'll love it!

**#2.** The Superfun Cowbell Overview Webinar

**#3.** Mystery BONUS! Better than mystery meat, guaranteed.

To get your free bonuses, go to thecowbellprinciple.com/bonuses and opt the heck in!

# 10. Confidence: How To Temporarily Lower Your IQ To Improve Your Success

Sometimes the dumbest idea is the best idea. In the "More Cowbell" sketch, Gene is portrayed as both a fool and a genius. What can we learn from that?

## Not Caring If Some People Think You're a Fool

Is there more to you? Maybe you aren't showing up fully in your work. Are you hiding your light? Maybe you're afraid to shine because you might attract the attention and derision that come with success. Or are you afraid you'll fail and look bad? It's not necessarily better to be mediocre and anonymous.

"Be yourself; everyone else is already taken." — Oscar Wilde

The cowbell guy, Gene Frenkle, is a fool. He doesn't care how he looks to people; he's giving them his cowbell, and the unfortunate combination of a short shirt and a huge stomach, because he loves the cowbell. He's so passionate he sometimes annoys even his friends and team members.

The Cowbell Player is a fool. SNL staff members have said the original sketch wasn't really funny until Will Ferrell put on the smaller shirt, increasing the sense that he was playing the fool. He is willing to look stupid if he has to in order to give people what they want. Other people think he's dumb or crazy but he's doing what he loves and getting great results from doing it.

To paraphrase from the SNL sketch, we don't have a lot of songs with cowbell in it. You'd "be doing yourself — and every member of (your team) too — a disservice if you didn't play the hell out of" your cowbell.

Even if you risk looking like a fool.

## Who Was That Masked Man? Are You Hiding Who You Really Are?

The lack of fear of what other people think of you gives you the freedom to excel. Fear holds us back; we're so afraid of the opinions other people have that we aren't willing to be ourselves. One of the reasons high school is so difficult is that people of that age are so afraid of what everybody thinks. That's why the high school play sucks. Garrison distinctly recalls high school sports being the same way. You have to go to school the day after the game and hear people say, "Hey, Wynn! You suck. You guys suck. Could you be worse?" (Well, we lost every game, so no, we couldn't be any worse.) Garrison was the quarterback, the leader of losers. It's the only time he ever lost, so it stood out.

The fear of being who you really are is what you should blame for your failures. If you're not being who you really are, then you have not achieved what you're meant for. Are you willing to be accountable for who you really are? Then take a look at the positive, high-potential parts of yourself that you're rejecting.

One thing that has made Will Ferrell famous is his ability to be ridiculous. How many comedians would have worn that shirt with that body in that sketch? In Anchorman he takes his shirt off and talks about the gun shows. Chris Farley's Chippendales sketch with Patrick Swayze is a similar example. Basically, what we're saying is you should get fat and take your shirt off.

On second thought, keep your shirt on, because what we're really saying is this: There comes a time in your life where you just have to be a fat guy in a tiny shirt. We're all fat now, except Africa.

So go that extra mile. Eat an extra pizza. Eat another donut. It's great for your career.

The thing that holds people back from who they could be, from who they should be, from who they are, is fear. It holds us all back. The best, most interesting things we could put in this book aren't in here because of what other people would think.

That's not true, of course. Or maybe it's a tiny bit true... but in general we do not shrink from speaking our minds for fear of others' reactions. Often the statements that some people object to are the ones that produce results. Garrison wrote in his recent book that no one reads the New York Times and that USA Today is the Fisher-Price newspaper, so the Washington Post wanted to talk to him immediately.

There's a difference between the archetypal high schooler (your inner high school snob) who sees you being a fool for your passion and the people whose opinion you care about. Typically, high schoolers don't help your career and they don't pay your bills… other people do. What do they think?

The red-headed kid with the cello at the bus stop is going to have a hard time in life, especially with dating. (Even if he becomes a world-renowned cellist, he'll probably still struggle with dating.) He might endure some bullying, but he's doing something to move his life forward. And even those of us who currently are not philharmonic players still know what we learned from learning an instrument. Full disclosure: During junior high, Brian kept his violin in his locker because he was too scared to walk around with it.

In our hearts, we all feel like that red-headed kid with the cello at the bus stop.

Confidence is not necessarily what creates success. It's projected confidence. We can be confident and not show it, and it doesn't work for us. On the other hand, you might cry in the parking lot beforehand, but if you walk in and project confidence, you'll succeed. And then, if you can project it, you might conclude that you possess it.

## How Could You Go Even Crazier? Stand Out. Be Unique.

When you let go and let it all hang out, you have a tendency to be really creative.

Brian and Garrison sometimes say stupid stuff, but in the end we come up with some good stuff we can keep. For example, here are four chapters that would have been extremely foolish to include in this book but that would have rocketed it to the bestseller list, at least in Finland:

• "How To Have Sex With Cracker Barrel Waitresses (Just Ask Them)"
• "What Can You Learn From Cults? How To Lead Tons Of Devoted Followers (Without The Mass Suicides!)"
• "How To Make Your Cheese Move (I Recommend Broccoli)"
• "More Anecdotal Evidence That I'm Successful"

And likewise, we dissuaded Malcolm Gladwell from releasing his new book More Information About Who You're Not and What You Can't Do About It.

## The Cowbell Principle Is About Your Individuality

It's much easier and more effective to be who you are than to be somebody else. And you'll find — if you're somebody else long enough, you can forget who you were.

If the idea of who you are is really disturbing to others, it's probably not who you really are; it's another mask. See Marilyn Manson. You may be trying to get attention or so afraid you're trying to cover it up.

Terry Bradshaw is someone who seems to have no reservation about looking foolish. And that's likeable. He'll look down at his notes and say, "I'm not going to read these." He's not trying to impress anybody. He's not "professional" but people connect to that. Charles Barkley has a similar charisma, because you never know what he's going to say.

## Stand Out by Being Ridiculous

People like ridiculous things because they like clarity. Often something is ridiculous because it is so exaggerated, which makes it identifiable and remarkable. As our culture becomes more and more saturated with social media and ideas and videos and news, people must become increasingly ridiculous to stand out.

Maybe you think Dennis Rodman is ridiculous, but there aren't many ex-basketball players who get invited to have lunch with the guy everybody thinks is going to blow up the world.

Exaggerate.

Gene Frenkle, the cowbell player, is a guy who seems to be unimportant but becomes the most important thing. Sometimes what turns out to be most important is something everyone thinks is trivial or dumb or whimsical.

Sometimes the fool is the wise man.

Perform the hell out of your cowbell, even if it makes you look like a fool.

Take this book, for example. Some may say it's a stupid concept, but we can't question the strong response we got from people. They loved the idea, so we wrote it.

Sometimes the best stuff is polarizing: Some people love it; others hate it. Good! It's better for you to have some passionate supporters than for everyone to ignore you because you don't stand out.

## Defy Mediocrity

If things are too vanilla, it's hard to be successful. However, the most popular flavor is vanilla. But that's because it's ice cream, something most people find hard to ignore. Vanilla wafers, not as popular. Vanilla Ice, not popular at all. We'll talk about him in the section of this chapter about being annoying.

Are you in an environment where people praise mediocrity? Then you might be incentivized to be mediocre, which will only assure you of an average career. Want a remarkable career? Become remarkable. Go and weird out some mediocre people.

What you achieve is to a degree about your expectations and the expectations of those around you. For example, a small percentage of families will not allow a kid to live at home after dropping out of college. They expect you to get a degree. They expect excellence. Dropping out of college is unacceptable to them. They paid for you to go, so you must succeed. No excuses. Some families are willing to shun their children if they fail. Right or wrong, this is pretty motivational for kids. Where excellence is expected, mediocrity is rare.

Mediocrity goes along with low expectations, a lack of motivation, a lack of ambition, and zero passion… it's sleepwalking through life. Is that what you really want?

A small percentage of people leave their jobs and create a business out of their personality. They don't have to invent a car or resell wholesale foods or split atoms. Successful speakers and consultants believe the power of their words and intellect is worth more than most things. Are these people confident? Definitely.

Some people succeed just because they want status; they want to look good and be acknowledged as special. Pathological? Maybe, but effective.

If you had $10 million, would you live in a private house on the ocean with huge walls around it? Sure, unless you really want the neighbors to see when you buy your wife that Lexus with a bow on it. Garrison once heard a guy say, "I bought my new Mercedes, and it came with tinted windows. What's the point of that if no one can see who's driving it?"

Sometimes your culture fights against your success. Brian learned when speaking in Norway that many Norwegians are fighting against a traditional cultural idea called Janteloven (pronounced yonta-loave-en), based on the laws of Jante, from, believe it or not, a novel. Why they let a novel hold such sway over them, we don't know!

These rules are so extreme that we want to share them with you, because when you read them we think you'll understand why the Norwegians need to rebel.

The 10 rules of Jante state:
1.    You're not to think you are anything special.
2.    You're not to think you are as good as we are.

3.    You're not to think you are smarter than we are.

4.    You're not to convince yourself that you are better than we are.

5.    You're not to think you know more than we do.

6.    You're not to think you are more important than we are.

7.    You're not to think you are good at anything.

8.    You're not to laugh at us.

9.    You're not to think anyone cares about you.

10.   You're not to think you can teach us anything.

Yikes!

Those rules make us want to punch somebody in the face (a very American reaction best carried out by anyone who has "rock" in their name, like Rocky, The Rock, or Jim Rockford). Or at least we want to make fun of these rules.

Americans don't believe that stuff, which is why the Scandinavian motivational company Speaker's Club imports American speakers. We feel bad that they have to fight that inside themselves, and we wish them all the best in fighting it.

But even Americans fight something similar, to a degree. When we succeed, even if we don't hear explicit jealousy from others, we can imagine it's out there. Your inner voice may ask you, "Who are you to deserve this or that?" And when we do succeed, we can feel a kind of survivor's guilt: "Is it bad that I've attained this or that when the people from my high school or college haven't?"

Still, we love humility, the kind you find among Tim Duncan's San Antonio Spurs teams; they are great, but their greatness comes from teamwork and good fundamentals. They never get too high or too low.

Brian's favorite definition of humility is this: a right-sized view of yourself, neither greater nor less than you actually are. Humility insists that we be honest, confessing when we're lucky but taking credit for the action we have taken and results we've achieved.

False humility is believing you are worse than you actually are. Egotism is believing you are better than you actually are.

If you're good at something, or even great at it, tell people. Or show them. Don't deny it. Don't hide it. Don't be embarrassed about it.

If you have gifts, talents, and skills, you have cowbells — and there are probably people with a fever for them. So go give them more cowbell.

## How to Finally Trust Yourself

As we began to write this chapter, Garrison observed, "I have never not trusted myself; but maybe I can't trust that." He's a pretty funny guy.

How often have you been wrong? Probably, like us, a fair amount. But have you had good intuitions on a regular basis? If so, then not trusting your own judgment would be terrible. Now, if you've found you don't have good insights and you've made a lot of poor decisions, then you actually have evidence that you shouldn't trust yourself. This can be an obstacle for anybody and can cause a loss of confidence. You need to investigate why you were wrong and how you can do better in the future. Check your ideas and plans with other people and get some feedback.

If your insights are always off, you probably have a blind spot, which could be based on a belief system, being in denial about something, or a self-esteem problem where you think you could never have the right idea. It could be that when growing up you were told you didn't know what you were talking about and that you were wrong. That'll sap anybody's self-confidence.

If you haven't been that successful, it's hard to have confidence because you don't have evidence of your ideas working out.

On the flip side, you can get over-confident due to a string of lucky breaks.

Ed Wood showed great bravery under fire in World War II. He believed he'd be okay no matter what, and he was awarded Bronze Star and Silver Star medals, mainly because he didn't get killed while doing crazy, courageous things. Afterward, he went into the movie business with that super-huge confidence. He made a bunch of terrible movies, earned terrible reviews, and died a penniless alcoholic. Had Wood lived in modern times, he might have made an excellent producer, but directing and writing were not his cowbells.

Ed Wood's cowbell was getting movies made (even ones that really shouldn't have been made). Posthumously he was credited with making what is arguably the worst movie of all time, Plan 9 from Outer Space (we can only imagine how bad the first eight plans were). Wood wrote, directed, produced, and often starred in his movies but lacked the overall talent and skill to succeed.

So you can be too confident or not confident enough.

Now, forgive us if we undo a bit of the humility we talked about earlier, but it's for a good reason.

You can be humble and have an accurate view of your value; but to move yourself forward, you might have to overestimate your abilities. Now that's a paradox!

The next section is meant especially for those who doubt themselves.

Being too honest with yourself can be counterproductive, because if it doesn't fire you up, it won't move you forward.

The No. 1 trait of the successful is they believe they deserve to win. They have the mindset "I ought to make more. I ought to be No. 1." They're driven to do it.

If you're 100% realistic, people might perceive you as being negative. For example, actuaries are people who deal with risk and uncertainty. They might tell you that given their ancestry and daily activities, they're likely to die at 73. That sounds pretty negative, even if it's realistic. Contrary to that, we hope that stem cells will enable us to be the first keynote speakers to live past 150. Now that's motivating!

The upshot is that you must have faith in yourself.

Trust yourself enough to believe you have the basic building blocks of success.

Living in all of us is the entire history of the human race and what we've accomplished. You and all humans possess much of the knowledge and natural ability and instincts that got us here. Yes, we've screwed up and killed a lot of people in the name of peace. We've screwed up the planet some. But we're still here. We don't have claws, we can't win hand to hand against a polar bear, we can't even outrun cheetahs, and we're still here.

Through thick and thin, war and floods and famine, human beings keep inventing ways to survive all the time.

Look at the progress we've made. Especially in the last 100 years. In 1869, we were perfecting suspension on a stagecoach. In 1969 we walked on the moon. As a species we have a great track record. You ought to trust yourself based on the mere fact that your genes come from human beings who prevailed over innumerable obstacles.

Don't second-guess yourself. Who are you to say that you can't do it? You are just one person who thinks he can't do it. Look at your ancestry. You've probably got relatives who walked across the entire country pushing a cart full of salt pork. Your great-grandma had 11 kids and cholera and ate crap.

Why does Des Moines, Iowa, exist? Settlers were trying to get to California. That's as far as they got. No one has Des Moines as a goal (no offense to people who are stuck in... umm, people who live in Des Moines).

Mary Kay of Mary Kay Cosmetics fame came from nowhere. She said, "You have to shoot for the moon so you at least end up amongst the stars" (which demonstrates her lack of education, because the moon is closer than the stars, and space is an instant-frostbite-inducing vacuum with no oxygen, but that's beside the point).

Make some calculated decisions. Most humans would sell themselves short. Even if that self-assessment were accurate, what good would that do? How can you be so unconfident about yourself, but super confident that you're right that you can't succeed?

There's no courage without fear. Go forward. Give it your best shot, like Pat Benatar.

There's only one way to achieve courage. You have to take action while you're afraid. Do that a few times and you'll develop what we call courage. In truth, people who succeed don't wait for courage. That's only in the movies. It's more accurate to say that heroes and cowards feel the same fear; it's the action they take that separates them.

## Sometimes the Dumbest Idea Is the Best One

We touched on this idea in the brainstorming section, and again at the head of this chapter. It bears repeating: Sometimes the dumbest idea is the best one. (Really? You want more of that thing that other guy thinks is totally stupid?)

"I'm telling you guys, you're going to want that cowbell."
— The Bruce Dickinson

Garrison once worked for Hendee Enterprises, a company that came up with industrial solutions. When one customer approached the company looking for a way to prevent moisture from getting into its paint vats, Garrison suggested a simple alternative to the warping, leaking covers the customer was using: "Why don't we put a giant shower cap on there and you can throw the caps away every day?" Five engineers said it was the dumbest idea ever, borne of Garrison's lack of education and understanding of the idea. But the covers had to be disposable because any wood or metal fabrication would warp or degrade. And caps made of special plastic and elastic wouldn't cause static electricity.

The customer bought 250 boxes of 500 covers each. Now every paint vat in the country is required to have this cover and it's sold in 30 countries. Not bad for a dumb idea, huh?

"I'm telling you guys, you're going to want that gargantuan shower cap."
— slightly modified by The Garrison Wynn

We often confuse simplicity with stupidity. If something or someone is simple, we think it must not be the best or most effective. Wrong! Sometimes an idea seems dumb because you're being dumb. Or snobby.

## Ignore the Snobs… For the Most Part

There's a big difference between what movie critics like and what the mainstream public will pay to see. In the 2000s, Brian often looked at Rotten Tomatoes to decide whether to see a movie, until he realized that he often disagreed with the critics whose reviews were featured on the site. Sometimes you want to see a mindless action flick, and most of those are disliked by movie critics. And some of the top-grossing movies are universally panned by the critics.

IMDB is a great resource, because it contains both mainstream viewer ratings and metascore, which is a measurement of critical response to the movie. If you're in the mood for something mainstream, ignore metascore. If you want to have a great time AND have your mind blown? Look for a movie that does well with both metascore (over 70) and high user ratings (above 7.0).

Movie critics are, at worst, snobs. They want something new and unpredictable, but often what people like isn't much different from what they liked 10 years ago. At best, because critics watch more films and think about them more than others, they have more insight than the average person.

What underlies snobbiness is nothing more than a kind of elite stubbornness. We have a way of doing things that has a tradition to it; it's the "right" way to do it. If you're doing something in a way other than that, we know it's not as good.

A snobby high school girl says, in essence, "My situation is far superior to yours. You can't make a contribution to me. By virtue of your birth, I should not even acknowledge your existence." What is this? Nothing more than a defense mechanism. High school is tough, so to look unafraid and invulnerable —to prevent people from bullying you — you look down on others first.

For us, the question is whether snobbiness — whether it comes from outside or inside ourselves — helps you create things that tons of people like. Sometimes, you definitely need to have standards. But sometimes snobbiness creates an intellectual paralysis that leads to creating things that only a small number of other snobs like.

One thing we're sure of: If your inner snob is causing writer's block, you need to exorcise that self-judging demon.

## Try Something Stupid

Is there something you've been afraid to do that you thought was a pretty good idea but you believe others would view as stupid?

Exercising through stupid ideas leads you to better ideas. Look at all the stupid contraptions we humans tried to fly in our quest to get airborne! Sometimes the only way to genius is through stupid.

We can guess that Formula 409 means the other 408 spray cleansers didn't work. Number 17 probably sprayed dirt onto dirt. And Fantastik may have had had an earlier version called Purty Good. "How's that clean?" "Oh, Purty Good… a lot better than Not Bad Spray!"

Are stupid ideas a good idea? Yes.

Since when is the first idea the best idea? If the first idea were indeed the best idea, then progress makes no sense.

## Be Willing to Be Crazy

Every city has some local dealership with a crazy commercial. If you were an intellectual, acting like that would kill your career, but nobody cares about the sophisticated furniture guy. Crazy Eddie Furniture beats that guy every time.

Mattress Mack is one of the most successful businessmen in Houston, Texas — so successful he once lost a $7 million football bet. In his commercials, he held a big wad of money and yelled, "We'll save you money!" Mattress Mack did, however, lose to chainsaw-wielding Hilton "That's a Fact Jack" Koch in a Conan O'Brien contest for most annoying advertiser.

If you're buying cheap local TV ads, it's good to be crazy. Crazy can be an advantage in certain other industries too; it depends on the market.

## How to Annoy People Until They Love You

As counterintuitive as it seems, annoying people and products get into our hearts and minds. They just won't go away, so we eventually give up and let 'em sink in. Some things you simply can't forget because they're so ridiculous or annoying, or both. Anything that's annoying has marketing power.

There's a fine line between annoying and fascinating. The Beatles' "Yellow Submarine" is a great song, but it won't get out of our heads!

Captain Kangaroo was horribly annoying but he had the No. 1 kids' show of its time. Barney was the same way. An astronomical number of parents had "I like you, you like me…" looping in their heads all day. How effective is Barney? He's a celebrity, despite not having much going for him. He sang awful songs, had an inane laugh. He really maximized what he had.

Fran Drescher of the sitcoms The Nanny and Happily Divorced earns a living because she's annoying. No offense to Miami, which we believe might be responsible for her. Or maybe it was Long Island.

It's okay to be annoying, and sometimes it's a cowbell! Irk people until they love you. Irk it out, irkface.

## ANDREA VAHL — GRANDMA TECHNOLOGY

Andrea is the coauthor of Facebook Marketing All-in-One for Dummies. She uses her improv comedy skills to blog as a slightly cranky character, Grandma Mary – Social Media Edutainer, at www.AndreaVahl.com. Here's her story…

My cowbell moment started when I realized I wanted to finally start my own business at age 39 and I wanted to incorporate my love of comedy somehow. Not too many years before, I had been laid off from a corporate job and taken some time to stay home with my young son. I had been learning the budding world of social media for a side business of in-home wine tasting. As I was doing so, I realized that there were very few funny tutorials on how to use Facebook, Twitter, LinkedIn, and YouTube for marketing a business.

I had always had a love of humor and had been doing improvisational comedy for eight years. I decided to take one of my improv characters (one I lovingly called Grandma Mary) and start a video blog with short, funny tutorials on how to use the social sites for marketing.

I had no idea that it would take off in the way it did. I was nervous to see how blogging as a character would be received in the "business" world and I have definitely found that Grandma Mary isn't for everyone. Some people think that dressing up as a character is strange and they don't relate to her. But so many other people found the tutorials funny and different that Grandma Mary, Social Media Edutainer, quickly grew a loyal following.

I truly believe that standing out and being different has been the key to my success. I grew my following and got a book deal (Facebook Marketing All-in-One for Dummies) all because I combined two things I loved: teaching and humor. Grandma Mary has a tribe of people who enjoy having some fun and like the creative approach to learning. I always make sure I'm delivering valuable information and a little inspiration with the tutorials. Grandma's message is "If Grandma Mary can do it, then you can do it too." I think that relates not only to marketing your business using social media but also to bringing your unique gift into the world. Don't be afraid to be different because it can be the key to your success.

## JESSIE SHTERNSHUS—HARNESSING THE IMPROV EFFECT

As the founder and owner of The IMPROV EFFECT, Jessie weds her lifelong passion for and expertise in applied improv with the fast pace and demands of the corporate world. She travels worldwide creating powerful learning environments for developers, designers, product owners, and many other teams, that will enable them to become better listeners, team players, problem solvers, innovators, and collaborators. Throughout her career,

Jessie has worked with companies such as Expedia, Getty Images, Skype, Pulte Homes, Celgene, Crayola, and Fidelity Investments. Her experiential sessions have been successfully implemented with startups, as well as Fortune 500 companies. Jessie has also been a speaker at conferences worldwide. Here's her story...

I organized The Improv Effect in Jacksonville, Fla. I started by teaching a basic improv class for beginners. The students kept coming back and invited their friends. Then they realized: These are skills we need at work. Improv skills are extremely helpful for work.

It was an effective way to market. My students were inside companies and could tell the boss what their company needed in their culture. I got paid to create my own sales force while having a ton of fun.

When people hear I do improv as a full-time job they say, "What?" After I do a workshop, the HR person sometimes asks, "How were you able to get everybody on board so quickly?" I take skeptical people who might hate training and get them in three minutes to go for the ride. I win people over quickly.

I can do that because of improv. It's about having empathy. I read the room and moment, and I play off what's going on. It helps that in the first three to five minutes, I can read the room and morph into what the room needs, playing whatever role is needed. I take improv students with me — the people who don't stick out like a sore thumb — because some performers are good but not aware of how they come across in a corporate environment. You can't be overly dramatic to software developers. You have to know how to mirror your audience. You have to understand the corporate world and its language. Don't act like some crazy "out there" actor. Step up and be expert or be sarcastic or not be in their face if they're introverted and nervous.

I get there early and scope out the room. Who is dominating the conversation? Who isn't talking? How is the person who hired me acting?

I did improv for so long that when interviewing for jobs, it was fun. I looked at it as an improv game —it was a scene with me and other people, and I didn't know what was going to happen. I found out everyone else hated interviewing, but it was a game to me because of those skills: listening, reading people, and thinking on the spot.

My parents signed me up for children's acting classes. I guess I was super dramatic. We learned improv games. I loved it, so I begged my parents to sign me up for improv and I never stopped. I love it because in improv, being different and creative is acceptable. You are validated for your own ideas; it's okay to walk a different walk. Finding improv before my preteen years gave me a lot of confidence.

I've always liked collaborating and an environment where we validate each other's ideas. I liked the people who were drawn to improv. They're witty, smart, clever, and interesting. They have an interesting way of looking at problems and life. They have a diverse way of life. Improv is like crack — the energy is fantastic.

I got into teaching because I did assisted teaching at Sunday school, and I taught at school for a couple years in my 20s. I liked the teaching but not the conformity of the school system. I loved watching people grow and gain confidence.

I'm still surprised I became an entrepreneur. I fell into it. I put a class out there to see what happened. Had I known too much about entrepreneurship, if I'd known ahead of time it just gets more difficult, I might have shied away. But I love it and wouldn't change it for the world. I like being challenged on a personal level.

I got into business training because people say, "We really need this. We're really struggling. Our team can't communicate, can't get along. We can't express ourselves." Some people said, "As a head of a company, I get thrown things unexpectedly and sound like a moron when I respond."

I did it slowly. I take risks but calculated risks. I test things. I did one class at a time. Let me tiptoe in and try it so I don't risk losing a lot.

Parting words? Listen and change. Laugh every day.

**How To Put Chapter Ten Into Action And Get The Results You Want**

- Are you ok with sometimes looking foolish to others? If not, go make a fool of yourself more often. Karaoke, improv classes or stand-up comedy open mics are great solutions for this.

- Write down 5 fears you have regarding other people. If you can't, get real, you're lying to yourself. Write them down anyway, you can burn the list immediately after.

- Are you afraid to be yourself?

- Who are some snobs or overly critical people you've listened to in the past? Now, in a private room, say this, "(their name) I'm not going to listen to you anymore. My own opinion is more important. Get out of my head. I own my life, not you. I believe in myself and my cowbell." It's important that you actually say it out loud.

- Come up with a name for your inner critic. Now out loud, say this, "(critic's name), here's how it's going to be from now on. When I want your opinion, I'll ask for it. Otherwise, I'm going to believe in myself. Thank you for your input- it's really valuable, but I'm in charge, not you."

- Are you ok with failing sometimes? If not, you need to fail on purpose more often- go back to the first question.

- What do you love that you're afraid to tell people you love? Tell some people. Stand up for your own interests. If they don't like it, tell them to get lost and find new people.

- Write a paragraph about who you are and how you're unique. Now, do you appreciate what's unique about you enough to be that with confidence?

- Thinking about who you are, what are 5 ways you could be yourself in an even more exaggerated way? Now actually do one of those.

- If you had to write a book about how to be you, what would its title be? Write 5 possible titles.

- Are there any areas where you might be overconfident? Could this come from an insecurity? What would a truly secure person do instead?

- If you could succeed at anything, what 5 things would you do? Which one do you really want to go after? Now take one action toward that goal.

- Write 5 semi-ridiculous unattainable goals down. Now which one do you think is actually attainable? Now take one action toward that goal.

**Hey You, Did You Get Your Free Cowbell Principle Bonuses?**
As the owner of this book (even if you somehow got it for free) you are entitled to some awesome bonuses!

**#1.** The controversial chapter they made us take out! "True Secrets of Success That Make People Uncomfortable" You may not want to read this one... it's very unconventional. But it's all so true that it's funny. And if you're the kind of person that just wishes people would level with you, you'll love it!

**#2.** The Superfun Cowbell Overview Webinar

**#3.** Mystery BONUS! Better than mystery meat, guaranteed.

To get your free bonuses, go to thecowbellprinciple.com/bonuses and opt the heck in!

# 11. How To Get What You Want And Make People Like It

Can your cowbell make you rich? In some cases, yes.

In the "More Cowbell" sketch, Bruce Dickinson says, "Babies, before we're done here, [the cowbell will have you] wearin' gold-plated diapers." What does that even mean? I'll tell you what it means.

If you're really good at something and you apply that in a direction where money exists, you get some of that money.

Bruce Dickinson knows what customers want and where that money is. What he directs you to do is going to give you a shot at that success.

Sharon Osbourne is a money-making machine. She organizes Ozzfest with no-name bands and signs them to contracts. Three or four of those bands do well each year, and she gets a percentage. Her approach combines profits and testing: She tests a lot of bands and takes a percentage from them for the opportunity. She promotes them a little (not too much) and doesn't risk too much. And she was uniquely positioned with the power to do it because she could say, "Ozzy really likes you and we want to sign you." If you're a metal band, Ozzy Osbourne is iconic.

We can glean a cowbell lesson from Ozzy himself, through statements he has made in interviews over the years. About the origins of Black Sabbath, the metal band he fronted, he professes they were an average band with nothing significant about them, other than their idea to play scary rock after seeing the movie Black Sabbath. No one was doing that kind of music at the time. With "good enough" talent, they became novel by playing up a unique brand that no one else had. Heavy metal took off.

So you can have a cowbell and do well; but if you can find some unique differentiator, it potentiates your cowbell. In other words, it makes your cowbell more powerful and next thing you know you're eating bats. And no one who eats bats is not successful. Being a little bit weird usually helps.

In short, you can take a cowbell that's not terribly original and add something else not original, and there you have a creative cowbell.

Ozzy also said he changed things up some with the times but never really deviated from the brand.

J.K. Rowling, who as of April 2014 has a net worth of $1 billion, struggled as a single mom who felt like a big failure as she sat down to pen the Harry Potter series. She had already been writing for 19 years and had the idea for Harry three years before, but a miscarriage and divorce left her contemplating suicide. She survived on state benefits while writing the novel. Motivation can come from surprising depths.

Hunger. Drive. Ambition. Passion. Some of it's already in you. Sometimes it comes from circumstances. Sometimes it's like a switch is flipped and you can't stand your life anymore and you're finally motivated.

### Is Your Cowbell Valued Where You Are?

You can be a great swimmer but if your high school doesn't have a swim team, you had better change high schools. Understand what people actually value and give it to them.

Being realistic about your skill level is important. How do you know you're good? You need proof.

Ed McMahon, who hosted Star Search for 12 years, said make sure before you come out to Hollywood you have actual talent. Otherwise it doesn't matter what you do here in Hollywood. You must have the kind of talent that would prompt people who do not know you to say you're good, because your friends and family are the worst judges of talent in your life.

In a way Blue Öyster Cult (remember, the band from the sketch? It's okay. Most people think the Blue Öyster Cult is a raw seafood bar) is a metaphor for your family and friends: Sometimes they say negative things. Sometimes they steer you wrong. Maybe that's why the lead singer has that kind of hair. They told him his hair was cool.

If you do have talent and a real cowbell, then get to the place where it's valued, work really hard, alienate your family… just kidding. But depending on who you have around you now, you might have to either ignore them or find new friends.

### Getting Honest About Sacrifice

Garrison's career and work cost him his marriage. He and his ex-wife continue to work together, but work definitely hurt the marriage. A lot of the biggest achievers make huge sacrifices that most people wouldn't. Many people, upon realizing their job interferes with their relationship, will trash the job. For some levels of success, more sacrifice is required. And hopefully, if that's your situation, you have a spouse and family and friends who support what you need to do.

So, it's not uncommon for people to lose marriages and friends while trying to make their cowbell pan out. It's about your level of willingness. Will Ferrell was willing to play the heck out of that cowbell. He sacrificed the feelings (and eardrums, and refined musical sensibilities) of the people around him to succeed. He earned the approval of the person who counted most — Bruce Dickinson —— because he wanted it, and because he loved that cowbell.

If it weren't for the sacrifices of people like Andrew Carnegie, John D. Rockefeller, and Cornelius Vanderbilt, America might not have become what it is, and we might not have won World War II. Vanderbilt donated his largest and fastest ship to the Union during the Civil War. The Rockefeller Foundation helped financially with WWI relief, and Rockefeller in his lifetime gave away roughly $550 million (the equivalent of $6.7 billion today). Carnegie not only oversaw the building of the massive U.S. steel industry, which in WWII was one of America's greatest cowbells, but he also gave away the equivalent of $4.6 billion. By the time WWII happened, the country displayed a spirit, spunk, and manufacturing power so strong that it overshadowed other factors and made our nation a powerhouse.

Now, you, not being a well-established business magnate, might not be positioned to dedicate billions of dollars to further the success of the thing you are passionate about. But are you willing to make some sacrifices? What a lot of people want to do is work a little, have a big lunch, come home at 5 p.m., and watch TV. Satisfaction may be the goal of the average person, but it's the enemy of greatness. The good is the enemy of the best.

If you're saying, "I don't have a cowbell. I'm just average," then you can't see your cowbell; ask other people what you're great at. Or you haven't developed a cowbell yet — so work on something you love that could eventually get you paid.

Everyone has a cowbell because we're all different. We all need each other and we specialize; that's why our societies can be so strong and why we dominate as a species. One question intrinsic to your cowbell is how useful do you want to be to humanity?

Animals go with instinct. Some can learn some things. We, on the other hand, are conscious of our situation. We can think. We're honest with ourselves. We grasp when we need to do something different. The human cowbell is understanding your circumstance and figuring something out.

## Why Willingness Is Indispensable

What can make the difference between riding on the trash truck and buying the trash truck (or trucks)? Sacrifice, willingness, and effort. If he really wanted to, the guy riding the truck could talk to people and figure out how to start his own waste management company. It's happened before! One guy saved a third of his pay for five years to buy a truck. He was the hardest-working guy and was willing to learn, and he exemplifies the idea that success is less a matter of social advantage and more a factor of particular attitudes (backed by effort).

Earlier in the chapter we mentioned the top trait found among the most successful: the belief that they deserve to succeed. From years of research, we've identified several other prevalent traits commonly found among people at the top, and a few of those traits recently surfaced in a list of success drivers (attitudes or abilities that push people to the top) identified by researchers and Yale Law professors Amy Chua and Jed Rubenfeld.

Although exceedingly successful people feel they deserve success, they often feel they haven't done enough to achieve that success. They also possess a willingness to forgo those of-the-moment desires so they can achieve goals they've set for the future. Chua and Rubenfeld call these three traits the triple package (which also serves as the title of their book on the topic). Wrapping these ideas in a nice neat bulleted list, we can observe these three success drivers as common among people who excel:

- A superiority complex — they believe they deserved to win;
- An insecurity complex — they felt their efforts were not good enough, which fueled constant improvement; and
- Impulse control — they resisted temptation enough to sacrifice the present for the future.

Even if you're not wired with those three traits or behaviors, you can learn from those who are. For the average person, the takeaways are these:

- Know you can win.
- Don't stop getting better because you have had some success.
- Be patient and look for the opportunities that will really get you where you want to go.

How do you become discontent with your efforts so you'll always want to be better?

Truly positive thinkers are rarely successful because they're easily blindsided by things they didn't see coming. Their mindset that it's always clear sailing indicates that they either are unwilling to look at obstacles or cannot bear the idea of them.

Time keeps on slipping, slipping, slipping... slipping away, as the Steve Miller band observed. So, what really matters is what you're practicing daily. It takes 10 years or 10,000 hours to produce something awesome as an expert in something. All that compound interest money stuff requires giving some money today.

Take some action every day. What you practice will increase. Everything you do today is an investment in something in our future, good or bad. For example, if you're investing in too much ice cream every day, you'll reap fat. If you're investing in good practices, you'll reap rewards.

If you're not at the point where you don't have enough time because life is too awesome, we hope you do get there. But it takes hard work for a long time.

## The Cowbell in Sports: Talent And Hard Work

Sports is a funny world like music in that there are a few individuals who make tons of money, a small group that makes a living, and then tons and tons of unpaid wannabes.

Want to be the best swimmer ever? Michael Phelps is your nemesis. A lot has been written about the reasons for Michael Phelps' success; he's the most successful athlete ever if you measure it by number of gold medals. Scientific American published an article that discussed his disproportionately long wingspan and double-jointed ankles. Phelps and his coach have attributed his success to mental toughness.

Why is Kobe Bryant so good? Talent? Talent plus hard work? Ray Allen is the best three-point shooter in the history of basketball, and his practice and work ethics are well documented. One of the things Allen Iverson is best remembered for is not how successful he was considering his relatively short height, but his disdain for practice. He made it to the finals but couldn't beat Kobe and company. His coach's criticism and his subsequent rant about practice made it clear he didn't believe in it.

Sports are impossible to talk about without theories and opinions, the kinds of things that have made a career for Bill Simmons, Stephen A. Smith, Charles Barkley, Kenny Smith, and others. That kind of debate is fun but perhaps pointless.

In sports, you're going to be born with a certain amount of talent. And you're going to have a certain work ethic (which you can improve). Some players are hungrier than others. And you're going to have some good luck or bad luck. Only the biggest freaks who make the biggest sacrifices are destined for certain championships.

Even without incredible physical gifts, players find ways to focus on one cowbell or another (maybe a three-point shot, maybe extreme ambition, maybe a dedication to defense) and can carve out a solid living in a major league.

## How Do You Balance Confidence With Not Really Being Good Enough?

Can you be honest with yourself and look at the limitations you have and the obstacles that can stop you? What's stopping you from being successful? Maybe you want to be CEO of a software company but you don't have a college degree. Realism says there's a low chance. Don't make the mistake of saying that Bill Gates did it, so anybody can and will. If that were true, everybody would be Bill Gates. Not everyone is.

Are you willing to pull off your rose-colored glasses to take a good hard look at the obstacles? If you are, you can build a path through the obstacles to success.

## How to Get a Positive Result from Negative Thinking

The start of any solution is a negative thought. In medicine, the first part of diagnosis is confusion and fact-finding. Most great discoveries happen in a time of fear and worry: World War II, the Cold War, the space race. People who are not happy with the status quo are the ones who make change happen.

You don't avoid the saber-toothed tiger by believing you'll be okay. If you're overly positive, you can be blindsided.

But let's distinguish between negative or critical thinking and fatalistic thinking. Negative, critical thinking — "What if this bad thing happened to me?" — is good. Fatalistic thinking — "Nothing good will ever happen to me" — is bad.

Negative thinking helps you come up with a plan for the saber-toothed tiger.

Positive thinking allows you to say, "Stop whining; things will get better," as you dive into the issues, planning to come up with answers.

## Degrees of Importance of Your Cowbell in Your Life

We've discovered that if something comes easily, we tend to devalue it. Maybe you do this too. For Brian, writing a book wasn't so hard, so he wondered, why do people think it's such a big deal? Because it is for most people! Your talents can create a blind spot. And because you devalue it, you might undercharge for it. Imagine how ridiculous it would be for Kobe Bryant or Michael Jordan or LeBron James to say, "Basketball is easy for me, so you don't have to pay me much for it." Prediculous! (Prediculous means so ridiculous it goes back in time and kills ridiculousness's grandparents.) The goal is to discover a talent and hone it and then get paid really freaking well for it.

Increasing your value takes time. Brian can now charge up to $250 an hour and feel like he's worth it. But if he were to say $300 he'd feel like he was getting away with something. Now, to someone who makes $20 an hour, this probably sounds stupid, arrogant, humblebrag or whatever. But it used to be he could only say he was worth $150 an hour. What changed? He got used to it and wanted more? When Brian was a kid in suburbia, he would mow the yard and get an allowance for that. His parents increased the allowance every year, which made him expect my wages to go up regardless of whether or not he did a better job. Maybe he was more experienced, but how much better can you really mow the lawn? There's a point of diminishing returns.

Brian learned from a couple of PR pros that you quote a high hourly rate to discourage hourly work; you want projects or monthly retainers instead. But this is likely a matter of preference. Projects and retainers can become inefficient and your hourly wage can drop quickly. On the other hand, if someone's paying Brian $200 to $250 an hour just to be on the phone giving his experience, opinion, or tips, and he didn't have to prep or follow up, that's really easy work. Like to talk? Get some expertise and credibility, market yourself, and get paid to do it.

But the other things that cause Brian's sense of value to go up are gaining more experience, getting better at what he does, being able to accomplish more in less time, and the fact that most people can't get paid fees like that 40 hours a week. So while $20 per hour might be $40,000 a year, $250 per hour is usually not $500,000 a year. More likely, it's $250,000. We've told you enough.

Speaking of which, we are incredibly secretive about how much we make. More people are willing to tell you what they weigh or how old they are than how much money they make. Why is that? If people shared facts about their income more, wouldn't it help the people who are undervaluing themselves? It might even curb the arrogance of those who are overvaluing themselves.

By the way, if by the time you talk to Brian his hourly rate has gone up, don't hate him. Be jealous of his cowbell. Very jealous.

"Nothing is as powerful as an idea whose time has come." — Victor Hugo

The X -Men was only for nerds for 37 years, but now they're worth more than $2 billion in worldwide revenue and more than $1 billion in profit. Their time has come.

## How to Get So Much Career Momentum You'll Always Have Work

Job Trends, Globalization, and Mediocrity

America has changed immensely since the 1970s and 1980s. Entire categories of work have disappeared because of globalization. The Internet has created jobs that didn't exist 20 years ago. Programming and Internet-related jobs are still on the rise.

China seems to be the future, and America is losing steam. Throughout history, there has been a long line of primary world powers: Britain, Spain, Rome, and Greece, to name a few. Is it the fate of Americans to follow the British? What can Americans do that can't be done better or cheaper elsewhere in the world? Not manufacturing. Perhaps not programming.

America still leads in some areas — the Internet, technology (more in software than in hardware), consumer goods, medicine (especially pharmaceutical), and entertainment. Some marketing is hard to outsource because it requires cultural and linguistic fluency. We are competitive in telecommunication, but other countries like Norway and Japan are at least as competent. And anything that can be more cheaply outsourced will either disappear from developed countries or at best become much less lucrative. Customer service is outsourced to a degree. Programming can be outsourced at a much lower rate to people in Pakistan, India, and other less expensive countries.

There are limited areas that offer job security for Americans. The people who earn this money will continue to finance the local support professions like construction, accounting, and food service.

The point here is this: As you identify your cowbell, consider whether it's something the people in your country will be able to pay for.

Endangered Jobs to Avoid

These are jobs noted to be vulnerable to outsourcing: call-center operators, customer service and back-office jobs, information technology, accounting, architecture, advanced engineering design, news reporting, stock analysis, and some medical and legal services.

Relatively Safe Jobs

Some jobs have a more stable prognosis in the States; maybe your cowbell fits well into one of these areas. Or, if you're not sure about your cowbell, maybe you can develop one that caters to one of these job categories. Either way, it's good to know that in America (until robots take over), there will always be:

- Schools, teachers, janitors, bus drivers
- Police, ambulance drivers, and firefighters
- People working in the jails and in law enforcement
- Nurses, doctors, medical technicians
- Government jobs
- Construction workers
- Grocery workers
- Garbage men
- People to make robots and repair robots until we make robots that can make and repair robots.

The point is not all doom and gloom, but don't be the person who was killed by the saber-toothed tiger because he didn't want to face reality! Think about what your cowbell is, and try to make it one that can beat your competitors not only in America, but all around the world.

## How To Put Chapter Eleven Into Action And Get The Results You Want

- How does your cowbell make you money? What are 3 new ideas for how it could make you more money?

- Who is competing with you for that money?

- What is your unique differentiator? What makes you different, if not better, than your competition?

- If you have a good brand, are you sticking to it?

- What are you willing to sacrifice to get where you want to be?

- Are you undervaluing your cowbell because it's one of the easiest things for you to do?

- Could your job be outsourced? Or done by a robot? If so, start looking for a career change and develop your skills, or become a robot.

### Hey You, Did You Get Your Free Cowbell Principle Bonuses?

As the owner of this book (even if you somehow got it for free) you are entitled to some awesome bonuses!

**#1.** The controversial chapter they made us take out! "True Secrets of Success That Make People Uncomfortable" You may not want to read this one... it's very unconventional. But it's all so true that it's funny. And if you're the kind of person that just wishes people would level with you, you'll love it!

**#2.** The Superfun Cowbell Overview Webinar

**#3.** Mystery BONUS! Better than mystery meat, guaranteed.

To get your free bonuses, go to thecowbellprinciple.com/bonuses and opt the heck in!

# 12. How To Discover & Develop Your Cowbell

To discover your cowbell, you'll need to answer some key questions. If you already like introspective writing, you'll love this. If you don't, and you're more of an extrovert, we recommend finding someone to talk this through with. Maybe you can take turns asking the questions and listening to each other's responses.

Here's the process. Each of these five exploration points has an associated set of questions:

1. What people want from you
2. Where you've failed in the past
3. Revisit what people want from you
4. What kind of person wants it
5. The best ways for you to give it to them

Let's address each of those in greater depth.

### 1. What Do People Have a Fever For – From You or Your Company?

If you're answering on a personal level, answer these questions:

- What is your unique gift that people need and want?
- What do they really seek out from you?
- What do people get from you that is hard to get anywhere else?
- How do you love to help people?

If you're looking for a business's cowbell, ask:

- What unique product or service do people buy from us?
- What do they pay for?
- What do we do differently from other companies that really means something to our customers?
- Why are we better than other companies?

If you draw a blank, ask your friends, family, and customers to help you answer these questions. If you still don't have any answers, think about what you'd like to get paid to do. You'll have a better chance of succeeding if it's something people generally pay for. You can try to go after something completely new, but just keep in mind you don't know if human beings will ever pay for it — you'll have to find out the hard way.

## 2. Where You've Failed In The Past
For an individual, answer these questions:

- What did you try in the past that failed?
- What did you think was your calling but it didn't work out or you hated it?
- What did you pursue only to find that too many others did it better?
- What have you dreamt of doing but haven't had the guts to attempt?
- How did you know you failed?
- Could you do it differently and perhaps succeed? How?
- Have you spent enough time thinking and writing about what you want to do?
- What have you learned from each failure? How can you apply those lessons now?

Brian wanted to be a rock star from ages 16 to 22 but failed by not doing enough to make it happen. He knew he failed because he didn't achieve it; he was jealous and depressed. He learned to pursue his dreams. It may not have been a failure to have such a huge goal that so few people achieve, but he failed by not pursuing medium- and short-term goals along the way to that bigger goal. He learned to pursue smaller goals. He learned to question what he was truly meant for.

Brian failed by not having a direction to pursue while working as a temp for several years. He learned to look for something he could get paid to do that he loved.

Brian failed by pursuing a career (acupuncture) that he soon realized he didn't actually want to practice. He was fascinated by how the topic could transform him and what he could get out of it, but he didn't think ahead to whether he would want to practice it. He learned he was more interested in discovering things that would work for many people than he was in just helping one person at a time.

Brian failed by pursuing something larger than what the company he was working for wanted. This happened in two companies. His mission was not aligned with theirs. He created more value for Fuel by optimizing and hiring and organizing, but that was as far as they wanted to go. He learned that his aspirations were bigger and maybe he was better freelance. As a consultant he can help companies optimize or grow to a point, and then they have cheaper internal people. He's a good small/medium-sized business catalyst.

He failed at the LinkedIn book because although it generated some interest, as a new book will, LinkedIn was not as big a topic. It wasn't as popular and upward trending as Facebook was when he wrote The Like Economy. He learned he should be writing about the big coming trend, stay ahead of it, figure out how, and then write about how. Content marketing and thought leadership are probably the thing to do now, if that's not too late. This book might be another mistake, but it's different enough from his other books that he's bound to learn something important from it.

This failure list taught Brian things about himself he might not have learned if he hadn't answered the above questions.

The fact is, you – fair reader – are messing up all the time, but are you learning from it?

If not, you'll keep making the same mistakes.

Who wants to do a failure list? That sounds horrible! But if you don't think you are failing, you are failing to realize you're imperfect. You are failing to learn from your failures.

This book could be also called "How to Stop Screwing Up in the Same Old Way."

## 3. Once More: What People Want from You

Given your perspective from the first two sets of questions, let's have you reconsider:

- What do people want from you?
- What will they pay you for?
- What gift do you have that's most valuable to others?

158

### 4. What Kind of Person Wants It?

Now that you know what you offer:

- Who wants it? What kind of people? What kinds of businesses?
- Who are they?
- How are they different from others?
- How can you find them?
- What else do they need?

You might find multiple types of people or businesses here, so answer for each separately.

### 5. The Best Ways for You to Give It to Them

For each type of person or company that wants what you offer:

- What are the best ways for you to deliver your cowbell to them?
- Where do you do it?
- How does it happen?
- What is that offering called?

It can be a long, strange trip. But the more you've experienced, the more you have to work with.

### Write Your Own Cowbell Story

Maybe you think you already know what your cowbell is. If so, here are a few questions to stimulate you as you develop your own cowbell story. You don't have to answer them all. They're designed to make your story complete and impactful:

1. What have you found that people want a ton of from you?

For a person: What is your unique gift that people need and want (and hopefully will even pay for)?

For a business: What unique product or service do people buy from you? What makes it better or different than what your competitors offer?

2. What was your journey or struggle in discovering it?

How was life or business before you found it?

3. What kind of person wants it?

4. What obstacles did you overcome to deliver it?

5. What was life or business like afterward? And can you put the effect into numbers?

But wait! What if you don't know what your cowbell is?! Yes, it's a journey, like life. But we'll try to help you find it faster with a few sets of questions.

What do you love to do?

## Make You "Stuff I Love To Do" List

1.    List 10 things you love to do. Don't even think yet about anything else. Just 10 things you love to spend your time on.

2.    Now look at that list. Is there anything there that helps other people?

3.    Are any of them things you do with other people?

4.    What role are you playing there (leader, motivator, listener, comedian, get-it-doner)?

5.    Is it a role that people can get paid for, even if you've never seen it sold before?

6.    How could you turn it into a business?

For example, maybe you love watching film noir movies. Start a blog about them. Make videos about them. Put ads on your blog. Repeat until your blog is popular and you're making money on ads. Then write a book about it. Or pitch a TV show about it.

Who do you want to be like?

Put that list aside and start another…

## Make Your "Who I Wanna Be Like" List

1.    What famous people do you admire?

2.    What qualities, talents, and skills do they have?

3.    What makes them so awesome?

4.    What makes them unique?

5.    What do they get paid for?

6.    Can you do that too?

7.    Can you do that in a smaller way or a different way?

8.    What's a manageable way to start on that?

For example, you love Oprah and Ellen, so you decide to start a small talk show in your church or community group. You get local Meetup groups to come see it by making the topic relevant to them and giving them a discount on the ticket price. You partner with a theater that needs more income from the days there aren't shows. You find fun and inspiring people to interview live. You make some money on the shows, take video, and start a YouTube channel with it.

**Mindset**

Find out what people have a fever for and give them more of it. What do people get really excited about?

1.    What if they want something that you don't? Are you here to serve you or them?
2.    What gets you excited? Who else gets excited about that?
3.    What bad things do people get addicted to? What not-quite-as-bad things do people get addicted to?
4.    For what things or people would you join a fan club? What Facebook pages have you liked? What conferences have you attended? Which clubs have you joined? Which TV shows do you watch religiously?
5.    What things do people do religiously?

What you can do

1.    Ask people questions.
2.    Search AdWords keyword tool.
3.    Look at which things people like the most.
4.    Look at top 10 lists.
5.    Learn what motivates people.
6.    Learn the science of addiction.
7.    Learn what drives people, including fears.

**What Is The Cake And What Is The Icing?**

Cowbell is the icing on the cake. People won't eat cake without it.

1.    What is the icing on your cake? Think about your business and what the fundamental services or products are. What small parts of that get people really excited?
2.    Ask your customers what their favorite thing about your product or service is.
3.    First tell your family, friends, spouse, parents, and kids you want to do a little experiment you got from a really dumb book you're reading. Then ask them what their favorite thing about you is.

You can spend endless hours journaling and trying to find yourself, but introspection is not as useful for finding a cowbell as retrospection is. Do something. Try things. Experiment. Get out there. Try dancing... parachuting, rock climbing, singing... and see if you can find that thing that you love, that you could be great at, and that someone would pay you for.

## How to Live at Full Wisdom

Ever make a mistake and realize you've already made that mistake before? This can be super frustrating, especially if you thought you'd already learned the lesson.

Brian thought he'd already learned to avoid picking the wrong person to be in a relationship with. But he entered into yet another relationship with someone (let's call her Megan, so we don't get sued) who turned out to have too many life problems to be functional at the level he wanted. She was too dependent on him.

Have you learned the difference between independence and dependence, and what the middle way is? Both independence and dependence are unhealthy. No man is an island. We need other people. But you can't let someone else be the entire reason for your existence. And adults should be able to stand on their own two feet. The middle path is interdependence — I take care of my fundamentals and my responsibilities, and you take care of yours, and we enjoy the best of each other, occasionally supporting each other in the worst.

The issue with Brian's girlfriend Megan was that she couldn't keep a job, she had serious health issues, and lingering emotional issues caused a life crisis every few months. Brian thought he'd learned to avoid relationships like that.

But he was blinded. She was the first woman he dated where every single guy who saw her privately told him, "She's pretty hot." She liked him, and he was done. He let her fill up an area of low self-esteem. He thought he'd learned to say no, but he hadn't learned to say no to someone this good looking. And he had a real soft spot for her weaknesses. It took a lot of suffering for Brian to say, "No, you need to take care of some of your basic responsibilities."

After they had broken up countless times, and she had dated their 45-year-old telemarketing boss because he had money, she warmed back up to Brian and asked him for money. That was the last straw. He set a boundary. She said, "Well, if you won't give me money, then you don't love me." Brian said, "Well, I'm sorry you see it that way." And it was over.

Some people say geniuses never make the same mistake twice. Well, when it came to relationships, Brian was Charlie from Flowers for Algernon — not exactly a genius.

Have you ever made the same mistake twice? There are ways to avoid that. And there are ways to consciously choose to learn more lessons from your previous experiences, if you want to take the time.

As we were writing the book and trying to figure out exactly what our cowbells were, Brian was also taking a screenwriting class, and the teacher gave them a tool called The Failure List.

The idea of the Failure List is to start writing down all your mistakes. And rewrite your failure list every day so that it's top of mind. When you do that, you're less likely to make an old mistake again.

That failure list, from the How to Discover Your Cowbell section, helped him see some mistakes he wasn't aware of and has helped him chart a better course for the future.

If you're willing to write about your failures and mistakes, and then keep them in front of you, you will avoid them in the future.

## Developing Your Cowbell

Is a cowbell more like a talent or a skill? It's a talent that you might have to develop skills for.

Some illustrations: A green thumb plus practice can make you a great gardener. Basketball talent plus practice makes you Tim Duncan, Michael Jordan, Kobe Bryant. Basketball talent without practice? Well, that's Allen Iverson.

How will you know when you're better? Take a minute and write down some potential milestones. What can you achieve with your cowbell? Identify something really specific, and attach numbers to it if you can.

Goals are not enough. They must be specific and short term. Long-term goals can be procrastinated. The goals that get done have a deadline.

Jerry Seinfeld used a very specific productivity habit to reach his level of success. Software developer Brad Isaac spoke to him back in the 1990s about how to become a great comic. Seinfeld said you have to create better jokes and the way to do that was to write every day. And how do you do that?

He told me to get a big wall calendar that has a whole year on one page and hang it on a prominent wall. The next step was to get a big red magic marker.

He said for each day that I do my task of writing, I get to put a big red X over that day. "After a few days you'll have a chain. Just keep at it and the chain will grow longer every day. You'll like seeing that chain, especially when you get a few weeks under your belt. Your only job next is to not break the chain."

"Don't break the chain," he said again for emphasis.

You may love your cowbell, but it's not always easy to make yourself do it every day. Create or adopt a system that helps you do it more, if not every day.

**Hey You, Did You Get Your Free Cowbell Principle Bonuses?**
As the owner of this book (even if you somehow got it for free) you are entitled to some awesome bonuses!

> **#1.** The controversial chapter they made us take out! "True Secrets of Success That Make People Uncomfortable" You may not want to read this one... it's very unconventional. But it's all so true that it's funny. And if you're the kind of person that just wishes people would level with you, you'll love it!
> **#2.** The Superfun Cowbell Overview Webinar
> **#3.** Mystery BONUS! Better than mystery meat, guaranteed.

To get your free bonuses, go to thecowbellprinciple.com/bonuses and opt the heck in!

# 13. I've Read The Whole Book-Now What?

Well, congrats, you read the whole book or at least proved you could flip to the last chapter. **Good job!**

Now what?

If you read the whole thing, you should know what a cowbell is, and if you did the exercises in the preceding chapter, you probably have a good idea what your cowbell is. **If not, answer the questions at the end of each chapter, you lazy fool!**

Now, fortunately, you agreed with everything we said about hard work, right? So you're ready to get to work? **Ok, go do something! (Like all the stuff at the end of the chapters.)**

Or if you're feeling lazy, reread the book. Or if you're really feeling lazy, fall asleep with some food on you.

And let us know how it goes!

Yours in authorship,
Brian Carter & Garrison Wynn
November 2014

# 14. Bonus: The Chapter We Were Advised To Remove

As the owner of this book (even if you somehow got it for free) you are entitled to some awesome bonuses!

**#1. The controversial chapter they made us take out!** "True Secrets of Success That Make People Uncomfortable" You may not want to read this one... it's very unconventional. But it's all so true that it's funny. And if you're the kind of person that just wishes people would level with you, you'll love it!

**#2. The Superfun Cowbell Overview Webinar**

**#3. Mystery BONUS!** Better than mystery meat, guaranteed.

To get your free bonuses, go to thecowbellprinciple.com/bonuses and opt the heck in!

# ABOUT THE AUTHORS

### Garrison Wynn
"Success is more than being good at what you do, it's about being consistently chosen to do it."

Garrison helps people make the jump from being great at what they do to developing the qualities it takes to be consistently chosen for the job. He gets them to understand why their products, services, or leadership styles—or those of their competitors—are selected. As he says, "If the world agreed on what's best, everybody would choose the best and nothing else would be considered. Decision making doesn't work that way." His presentations help people become more influential regardless of circumstances.

Garrison has presented to some of the world's most effective leaders and business developers, from multibillion-dollar manufacturers and national associations to top New York Stock Exchange wire houses. He has a background in manufacturing, instrumentation, telecommunications, financial services and is a former professional stand-up comedian. In his teens, Garrison worked with Magnavox and baseball legend Hank Aaron to promote the world's first video gaming system, and by age 27 he became the youngest department head in a Fortune 500 company's history. He researched and designed processes for 38 locations nationwide and developed and marketed products still being sold in 30 countries.

Garrison is the author of the Amazon.com bestseller The REAL Truth About Success, has contributed weekly to The Washington Post, and has coauthored with Stephen Covey. He is also a chemical plant explosion survivor who helps organizations communicate safety more effectively. His award-winning success tools receive high praise, but his greatest strength is a magnetic live performance that keeps him in high demand, with more than 600 inquiries and 100 speaking dates per year.

**For more about Garrison, go to**
**http://www.motivational-speaker-success.com/**

## Brian Carter
"I love quotes so much!"

Brian Carter, internationally bestselling author of three books: The Like Economy, LinkedIn for Business and Facebook Marketing, is one of the best known names in digital marketing and social media and is respected as an international authority on how organizations can generate bigger business results. His 18 years of business success guide The Carter Group, which strives to provide the best possible service and results in the digital marketing industry.Brian has keynoted and developed marketing programs and strategies for companies of all sizes, including Microsoft, Universal Studios, The U.S. Army, The World Health Organization, NBC Universal, PrideStaff, PediaCare, Chloraseptic, Dramamine, Hardee's and Carl's Jr.

Brian has been interviewed by Bloomberg TV, Mashable, The Wall Street Journal, Forbes, ABC News, Information Week, U.S. News & World Report, Inc. Magazine, and Entrepreneur Magazine.

Brian has written for many top marketing blogs including Social Media Examiner, Mashable, Convince & Convert, Search Engine Journal and AllFacebook. He has an overall reach of more than 150,000 fans through Facebook, Twitter, LinkedIn, and his other marketing channels. He has taught more than 10,000 students. Brian has spoken at top marketing conferences including Social Media Marketing World, Moz, SMX, Pubcon, The AllFacebook Expo and Socialize and the American Marketing Association.

His hands-on business experience, cutting edge insights, background in improv and stand up comedy culminate in a keynote speaker and trainer who leaves every audience not only entertained, but armed with powerful strategies and tactics. Brian is a seasoned expert and most entertaining presenter in Internet marketing.

### For more about Brian, go to
http://briancartergroup.com/

And one more thing…

**Hey You, Did You Get Your Free Cowbell Principle Bonuses?**
As the owner of this book (even if you somehow got it for free) you are entitled to some awesome bonuses!

> **#1.** The controversial chapter they made us take out! "True Secrets of Success That Make People Uncomfortable" You may not want to read this one… it's very unconventional. But it's all so true that it's funny. And if you're the kind of person that just wishes people would level with you, you'll love it!

> **#2.** The Superfun Cowbell Overview Webinar

> **#3.** Mystery BONUS! Better than mystery meat, guaranteed.

To get your free bonuses, go to thecowbellprinciple.com/bonuses and opt the heck in!

That's us practicing that whole "annoying" principle.

☺

Made in the USA
Lexington, KY
17 October 2016